Presidential Cars & Transportation

From horse and carriage to Air Force One, the story of how the presidents of the United States travel.

By William D. Siuru, Jr.
& Andrea Stewart

Published by

 **krause
publications**

700 E. State Street • Iola, WI 54990-0001
Telephone: 715/445-2214

Please call or write for our free catalog of automotive publications.
Our toll-free number to place an order or obtain a free catalog is 800-258-0929
or please use our regular business telephone 715-445-2214
for editorial comment and further information.

Library of Congress Catalog Number: 95-76860
ISBN: 0-87341-341-5
Printed in the United States of America

ACKNOWLEDGEMENT

Charles G. Barnes, Little White House Historic Site

Jim Benjaminson, Plymouth Owner Club

Calvin Beauregard

Jean Caldwell, Technical Services Librarian, American Automobile Association

John Conde

Chrysler Historical Collection

Daniel, Mann, Johnson and Mendenhall

Robert Denham, Studebaker National Museum

Jonathan Elkins, JMPR Public Relations

Dan Erickson, Ford Photographic

John Gunnell, Krause Publications

Charles Harrington, Cadillac Public Relations

Imperial Palace Hotel and Casino

Charles Jensen

Lu Knox, archivist, Forbes Library

Brian Lee

Mike McDonald, Professional Car Society

Larry Mitchell, AMC World Clubs

Marsha Mullins, Curator of Collections, The Hermitage: Home of Andrew Johnson

Museum of Automobiles, Petit Jean Mountain, Arkansas

Bill O'Gara, O'Gara-Hess & Eisenhardt

Pate Museum of Transportation

Gerald Perschbacher

Public Affairs, Lincoln-Mercury Division

Public Affairs, 89th Military Airlift Wing

Public Affairs, Marine Helicopter Squadron One

Public Affairs, United States Air Force

Stella Pytrek-Blond, The Packard Club.

Edward J. Russo, City Historian, Lincoln Library

H. Terrence Samway, United States Secret Service

Harry Simpson

Alice M. Starke

Mary Story, Cadillac Public Relations

Todd Strand, State Historical Society of North Dakota

Bernard J. Weis, Editor, *Pierce Arrow Society*

World Classic Auction & Exposition Company

TABLE OF CONTENTS

INTRODUCTION

Presidential vehicles and motorcades have changed significantly since the days when President Woodrow Wilson rode in an ordinary open car procured locally during a visit to Bismarck, North Dakota. (State Historical Society of North Dakota)

Today, the president of the United States may work in the Oval Office in the morning, give a speech in California in the afternoon, and prepare for the next day's meeting with world leaders in an Asian city aboard "Air Force One." Presidential travel has changed drastically from the more leisurely days of the 19th century when the president rarely left Washington.

Relative to his predecessors, the 19th president, Rutherford Hayes (1877-1881) was known as "Rutherford the Rover" because he traveled so much. Rutherford was the first sitting president to visit the West Coast, then a rather arduous train trip. Likewise it was not until the 28th president, Woodrow Wilson (1913-1921), that a president crossed the Atlantic Ocean while in office, then a rather time-consuming, though leisurely trip by steamship. Previously, Theodore Roosevelt (1897-1901), the 26th president, was the first president to leave the United States when he traveled on the U.S.S. Louisiana for an inspection tour of the Panama Canal. Alaska was not visited until the 29th President, Warren G. Harding (1921-1923).

Today the president's transportation fleet consists of several presidential limousines, special Boeing "jumbo jets" at nearby Andrews Air Force Base and a Marine Corps helicopter that can land on the White House lawn; all stand ready to take the president anywhere he needs to be. This is a far cry from the days before William Taft (1909-1913), the 27th president, when the president had to supply his own horses and carriages. Often these were gifts from generous private citizens. Even when presidents traveled in luxurious, private railroad cars, these were usually owned by railroad magnates.

In addition, transportation on Inauguration Day has changed drastically. Up until 1921, when Warren Harding rode to his inauguration in a Packard Twin Six, horse-drawn carriages were used, with a few exceptions. Thomas Jefferson (1801-1809), the 3rd president, walked the one block to the Capitol when his son-in-law, Jack Epsfield, failed to show up with the carriage at the scheduled time. Jimmy Carter (1977-1981), the 39th president, hiked 1-1/2 miles from the Capitol to the White House during his inaugural parade, but that was a personal preference.

There have been some unusual forms of presidential travel. Teddy Roosevelt was the first president to submerge in a submarine. In August 1905, he stayed underwater for an hour aboard the U.S.S. Plunger. Harry Truman (1945-1953), the 33rd president, repeated the feat when he submerged in an enemy submarine, the former German U-boat, U2513. This occurred near Key West, Florida.

PRESIDENTIAL TRANSPORTATION FIRSTS

[While in Office]

FIRST	PRESIDENT	DATE	EVENT
Travel by steamship	James Monroe	May 1829	Rode on S.S. Savannah
Travel by train	Andrew Jackson	1833	12-mile trip
Ride in an automobile	Wm. McKinley	1899	Rode in a Stanley steam automobile
Travel by airplane	Franklin Roosevelt	Jan. 1943	Traveled on "Dixie Clipper"
Travel by helicopter	Dwight Eisenhower	Sept. 1957	Short trip on a USMC UH-34 helicopter

Source: *The World Almanac of Presidential Facts* by Lu An Paletta and Fred L. Worth.

Transporting and protecting the president go hand-in-hand. Before the turn of the century, both were quite simple. Even after the assassination of President Lincoln, the president moved around Washington with relative ease. Some presidents rode horses or drove their own horses and carriages. The Secret Service, established in 1865 as a division of the U.S. Treasury Department to fight widespread counterfeiting during the Civil War, was not assigned the job of protecting the president until 1901, after the assassination of President McKinley

Through the years, the Secret Service's protective role has been expanded to cover many other people in the presidential circle.

EXPANSION OF THE SECRET SERVICE'S PROTECTION

1901 President
1913 President-elect
1917 Members of the president's immediate family
1951 Vice-president
1965 Former president and spouse
1968 Spouses of deceased presidents until their remarriage and children of former presidents until age 16
1968 Major presidential and vice-presidential candidates
1971 Visiting foreign dignitaries
1974 Vice-president's immediate family
1976 Spouses of major presidential and vice-presidential candidates

The president is most vulnerable when the Chief of State is traveling by limousine. Therefore, the president's motor travel has changed significantly from the days when the president often traveled in the back seat of a phaeton with the top down. The number of road trips has been greatly reduced by using "Marine One," the presidential helicopter, which can carry the president on the shorter hops from the White House lawn to Andrews AFB, Camp David for rest and relaxation or to many other locations in the vicinity of Washington. Also personal contact with the public has been reduced. While still visible, the president usually remains "buttoned up" inside the presidential limousine where hand-shaking opportunities are limited.

Motorcades present some real challenges for the president's Secret Service guards. The agents meticulously check the parade route before the trip. A Secret Service "advance team" goes to out-of-town destinations seven to ten days ahead of the president. Working with local law enforcement agencies, they plan security in minute detail and map out the safest route for the president. Prior to the motorcade, sewers are checked for bombs, while manhole covers and potential locations for snipers are inspected. Nothing is left to chance. During the motorcade, agents augmented by local police are posted along the route. Counter-sniper teams take up strategic locations on top of and inside buildings. Buildings are secured and strict crowd-control procedures are put into action.

The president's Secret Service "bodyguards" surround his limousine when it is moving a slow pace through crowds. When the motorcade speeds up, the agents move back to the follow-up cars, following the presidential limousine within a close proximity. For years, specially built four-door Cadillac or Lincoln convertibles were used for follow-up duties. In recent years, the president's protectors have used vehicles that provide them with more protection. Today, you will see some formidable looking General Motors-built Suburbans equipped with 454 cubic inch displacement (cid) V-8 engines with obvious bulletproofing and armoring serving as follow-up vehicles. Incidentally, these "Suburban 454s" are also used to follow "Air Force One" while it taxis on the tarmac.

Today the president travels in a specially built limousine protected by the latest armoring and bulletproofing technology. (U.S. Secret Service)

Typically, two armored presidential limousines are maintained at all times. One might drive the president to the destination point, while the companion vehicle follows, serving as backup. Two limousines are also used to add deception to the Secret Service's bag of protective tools. Sometimes both are used in a motorcade, one being a decoy. When the president and first lady go to a restaurant, for instance, they might arrive in one limousine at the front door and leave in a different limousine via the rear door.

Communication technology used in presidential cars is a closely guarded secret. Aides on board the president's and follow-up cars may be from a wide variety of governmental agencies. Agents communicate between cars, as well as with agents along the route, stationed on rooftops, at intersections and even in sewers.

When the president is ready to leave the White House, he notifies his military aide, who calls the White House usher, who calls the Secret Service Garage, which brings the car to the door. The "black box" containing the codes necessary to launch a nuclear strike is then brought on board. Once POTUS (codename for the President Of The United States) gets in the car, a "trip message" is flashed to every agency involved in the journey, as well as those that require constant knowledge of the president's whereabouts. Among these are the Joint Chiefs of Staff, Stragetic Air Command, CIA and the National Security Council. Presidential communications use restricted radio frequencies as well as voice and data scramblers to maintain security for on-board radios, phones, and computer/fax machines. There is so much electronic gear that a trickle charger is kept hooked up when the car is not in use to avoid draining the battery.

No matter the extent of the protection provided, the safety of the nation's Chief Executive cannot be absolutely guaranteed. John F. Kennedy wisely stated less than a month before his assassination that no amount of protection would be enough if anyone had "a willingness to trade his life for mine."

CHAPTER I

BEFORE CARS AND PLANES

PRESIDENTIAL TRAVEL IN KINDER AND SIMPLER DAYS

In earlier days of the United States including the early part of this century, life was far simpler for everyone including the president of the United States. He moved around freely in Washington and visited the rest of the nation at will, though rather infrequently. From George Washington until the assassination of William McKinley in 1901, the president was pretty much free to come and go as he pleased without an entourage of Secret Service agents. But the presidents' early journeys were not without their hindrances. The poor condition of the nation's roads, especially in rural areas, and the lack of advanced machinery made any journey long, tedious and often uncomfortable. Therefore, most of the presidents who served during America's first century or so stayed fairly close to Washington.

HORSES PROVIDE PLEASURE AS WELL AS TRANSPORT

The usual means of transportation for those early presidents of course was the horse. It was not at all unusual to see Thomas Jefferson (1801-1805), a lover of horses, riding on horseback around Washington. President Jefferson rode as much as 40 miles a day while in office. Back then the job of president was far less demanding, leaving him more time for leisure activities. Five days after leaving office in March 1809, ex-President Jefferson mounted one of his favorite horses and rode the 140 miles through snow and sleet back to his home at Monticello.

When James Monroe (1817-1825) took office, the renovation of the White House was not quite completed. It had been burned by the British during the War of 1812. With the plaster still fresh and the paint still wet, the Monroe family found the condition of the White House damp and disagreeable. Since the Monroe's estate at Oak Hill was far more comfortable, they stayed there until the White House was ready. Like many ordinary work-

William McKinley had the distinction of being the first president to ride in a car. His last ride was also in a horseless carriage. In 1901 this electric ambulance delivered McKinley to the hospital after he was shot by an assassin.

ers today, President Monroe stayed in Washington during the week and went home for the weekend. This meant a 33-mile commute on Monday and again on Saturday mornings by horseback.

John Quincy Adams (1825-1829) also loved to ride. He would generally awake between 4 a.m. and 6 a.m. so he could take a leisurely horseback ride before attacking the day's work. But his horses may not have enjoyed the rides quite as much as the rider, as evidenced by a couple of incidents: In 1825, one of his horses fell while climbing Bull's Neck Hill and died; and in 1828 a pony threw Adams, resulting in a painful neck injury to the president.

Andrew Jackson (1829-1837) was another avid equestrian as attested to by the famous statue located in Lafayette Park across the street from the White House. This statue depicts Jackson in military uniform mounted on a horse. Like so many other presidents he kept running horses in the White House stables. He also frequented local racetracks to watch Emily, Lady Nashville and Bolivia, his fillies, race.

William Henry Harrison (1841) had an even more disastrous horse ride that would actually contribute to cutting his presidency short--very short. Although Harrison was presented with a fine coach for his inauguration, he chose to ride his favorite horse, a white charger, through the bitter cold to the Capitol. This horse ride, followed by his two-hour long inaugural address delivered in freezing weather, resulted in Harrison coming down with pneumonia and dying a month later. President Harrison has the distinction of being the first president to die while in office, as well as still being the president who served the shortest term: less than a month. His wife, Anna Symes Harrison, never even got to move into the White House. Incidentally, President Harrison also has the dubious honor of being the first president to ride a train after his death. His funeral train carried his casket from Washington, D.C. to Columbia, Pennsylvania.

Zachary Taylor (1849-1850), another horse lover, let "Old Whitey," his favorite horse and war companion, graze on the lawn of the White House. The horse's presence was quickly noticed by guests of the White House at outdoor receptions held on hot summer days. Later, Old Whitey, with stirrups reversed as required by tradition, walked close behind the president's body during Taylor's funeral procession. President Taylor, too, had a short time in office, a little over a year, when he died of acute gastroenteritis. He had eaten raw fruit washed down by cold water

President Franklin Roosevelt, Eleanor Roosevelt and a couple of friends about to take a ride at the "Little White House" in Warm Springs, Georgia. (Little White House Historic Site, Georgia)

and iced milk after attending a Fourth of July celebration at the Washington Monument. Incidentally, in 1850 the Washington Monument was still under construction.

President Ulysses S. Grant loved to ride, but an incident during one of his rides in Washington got him into trouble with the law. While spurring on Julia, his favorite racehorse, to go faster down M Street between 11th and 12th in Washington, the president was stopped by police officer William West. Officer West, surprised at who he had apprehended for speeding, was willing to let the distinguished rider go. But President Grant asked him to treat him like an ordinary citizen. Grant accepted a ticket, and paid the $20 fine--a princely amount for the day--on the spot.

After the president began to regularly travel by train, automobile and even the airplane, several presidents continued to ride just for recreation. For instance, President Woodrow Wilson (1913-1921) took up riding a horse, named quite appropriately Democrat, on doctor's orders as part of his recovery program after a serious illness. Even though crippled by polio, Franklin D. Roosevelt (1933-1945) loved to take horseback rides often accompanied by his wife while at his "Little White House" in Warm Springs, Georgia. Such rides required that he be hoisted into the saddle. Ronald Reagan (1981 and 1989) who spent some time in the saddle in his movie days, often rode a horse around his Rancho del Cielo (Ranch in the Sky) near Santa Barbara, California.

Even though crippled by polio, FDR loved to ride. (Little White House Historic Site, Georgia)

HORSES AND CARRIAGES

Unlike the elegant and elaborate horse-drawn carriages and coaches used--and indeed still used--by European royalty, the carriages of the U.S. presidents were usually no different than the ones used by contemporary, ordinary American citizens. Then again the holders of the nation's highest office were usually pretty ordinary people, at least before the media blew them up to be bigger than "life size." Presidents were not royalty, and several presidents went to great pains to ensure they were not treated as royalty. Those presidents who occasionally strayed from plain to ornate conveyances often would be brought back to reality when they were chastised by their contemporaries and in the press. Even in modern times, the design of the highly specialized vehicles used by presidents has been driven more by security considerations than for ostentatious purposes.

In fact because these carriages were so ordinary, few thought them worthy of preserving. Unlike the many presidential cars and airplanes, few complete carriages used by many of the early U.S. presidents still exist. Often only faded paintings, photographs or bits and pieces tell us how presidents traveled in the horse and buggy era.

George Washington (1789-1797) traveled from his home at Mount Vernon to New York, then the Capitol of the United States, for his first inauguration in 1789. For longer journeys, he traveled like most people of the day--in a closed carriage. The carriage was pulled by a team of fast horses that were exchanged with fresh ones at each post along the way to complete the long journey.

On special occasions, President Washington used a coach belonging to his wife, Martha, that was a gift from the Pennsylvanian state government. The cream-colored carriage was decorated with the Washington family crest and oval panels depicting the four seasons. The gilded "Penn Coach" drawn by six white horses was a regal sight, a fact that did not go unnoticed by Washington's critics. They felt the carriage was much too elaborate for the head of the new country, founded because of the tyranny of a British monarchy that rode in fancy coaches. Washington, a bit uncomfortable with all the grandeur, stated he preferred his coach to be "plain and elegant" rather than "rich and elegant."

In 1791, Washington made a presidential tour of several of the "southern" states, a journey not taken lightly. Accompanied by Thomas Jefferson and Henry Knox, the entourage included, as noted in Washington's diary, a "Chariot and four horses.... a light baggage Wagon and two horses--four saddle horses besides a lead one for myself..." The latter was Washington's old white charger.

Where Washington's six-horse "Penn Coach" was on the elegant side, his successor, John Adams (1797-1801), used a coach drawn by only two horses. He did not want to "excite popular feelings and vulgar insolence for nothing." President Adams even insisted that his wife, Abigail, remove the Quincy family coat-of-arms from the doors of her carriage. He thought the logo a "trifling symbol of aristocratic pretension."

The James Madisons (1809-1817) had a simple carriage for daily use, but used a far fancier coach for special occasions. The charming society-minded first lady, Dolley Madison, enjoyed driving around Washington in style using a rather fancy coach. When British soldiers set the White House on fire during the War of 1812, Dolley hastily loaded up that carriage with important state documents, White House silver, and the famous Gilbert Stuart portrait of George Washington. Then she drove the loaded carriage across the Potomac River, carrying the priceless possessions to safety in Virginia.

President Andrew Jackson was also criticized for sometimes forgetting America's democratic ideals by riding in his fancy formal carriage that was upholstered in red crushed velvet and was pulled by a team of white horses. The quite controversial Jackson, sometimes called "King Andrew," also spent lavish amounts for the time of over $50,000 to redecorate the White House, including over $4,300 for a sterling silver dinner and dessert set. Just before leaving office, some 60 of "Old Hickory's" friends and political associates presented Jackson with an elegant phaeton made from the timbers of the U.S.S. Constitution. Paintings on either door panels depicted "Old Ironsides" under full sail. This carriage drawn by four of Jackson's finest horses was used for the inauguration of his successor, Martin Van Buren (1837-1841). Starting a long tradition, this was the first time both the outgoing and incoming presidents rode in the same vehicle on Inauguration Day.

13

This photo taken around 1875 shows Andrew Jackson's Brewster carriage on the left, which was used for official and and social functions. President Jackson also used the carriage several times to travel between Washington and The Hermitage, his estate in Tennessee. On the right is his phaeton. (The Hermitage: Home of Andrew Jackson)

President Martin Van Buren (1837-1841) was a sight to behold traveling the streets of Washington in an olive green coach. This coach with liverymen in color-coordinated uniforms was pulled by a team with silver harnesses and a coachman riding in the box up front. Such a display did not go unnoticed by his political adversaries who considered this as evidence of extravagant and luxuriant living.

Just as today, the presidents sometimes could do no right. When the John Tyler (1841-1845) family first moved into the White House in 1841, they owned a second-hand carriage. President Tyler was criticized for having used the old carriage for over a month before finally having the previous owner's coat-of-arms painted over. But not long after the inaugural, the Tylers would be traveling about Washington in the grandest style with a fine coach complete with liveried coachmen and footmen. In fact, Mrs. Tyler would eventually be ridiculed for driving with four horses that were "finer than those of the Russian minister."

Much of the controversy and public ridicule surrounding the presidents' choices in carriages stems from the fact that prior to 1909, the presidents had to supply their own horses and carriages from personal funds. Great extravagance was considered a sign of frivolity--while ordinary choices signified cheapness. It was not until William Howard Taft's (1909-1913) administration that money was appropriated for presidential vehicles.

Several presidents were offered gifts of horses or carriages from influential friends or groups. Sometimes personal ethics kept them from accepting the generous gifts. President Andrew Johnson (1865-1869) returned such an offer from a group of New York bankers and merchants, suggesting that it was not correct for a president to accept gifts. President James K. Polk

(1845-1849) received two such offers--one a fine riding horse from an admirer, the other a luxurious carriage from a group of citizens--but declined them both, thus discouraging any further offers. President Grover Cleveland (1893-1897) was so honest that he measured the hay in the stables when he assumed office and sent a check to ex-President Chester A. Arthur (1881-1885) for it.

But many presidents accepted the gifts, and they did not necessarily lose their ethical standing for doing so. Even Honest Abe accepted a plain but elegant barouche upon his first inauguration from a group of New York merchants. The carriage rounded out the Abraham Lincoln (1861-1865) collection to three carriages, all of them far more modest than those of the Madisons and Van Burens.

There were many tragedies while the Lincolns occupied the White House. Among them was when the brick stable, then located between the Executive Mansion and Treasury Department, burned to the ground as the Lincolns watched one February night. All the animals in the stable were destroyed, including the president's horses and two ponies belonging to young Tad Lincoln. Three carriages did survive, including the elegant barouche that would carry President Lincoln to the Ford Theatre on the tragic night of his assassination by John Wilkes Booth.

President Theodore Roosevelt (1901-1909), a devoted horseback rider, tried to hold back the modern tide, stating, "I came to the inauguration in this horse-drawn vehicle and I will leave in it." Horse-drawn carriages would be used until the inauguration of Warren Harding in 1921. Even today, the president's or ex-president's last ride is usually in a black caisson drawn by six matched gray horses followed by the presidential flag, riderless horse and an assemblage of world leaders.

RIDING THE RAILS

Presidential travel would change significantly as twin rails of steel were laid across the country. In 1827, the Baltimore and Ohio Railroad was chartered and within two years, 14 miles of double track had been laid. The first locomotive to run on a public railway was the Delaware & Hudson's "Stourbridge Lion" that traveled along a 16 mile section of track in 1829. In the same year, the first real mainline railway was put into operation by the Baltimore & Ohio. Peter Cooper's famous locomotive, the famed "Tom Thumb," was the line's first locomotive. Incidentally, the name "Tom Thumb" was chosen because the locomotive was tiny with a boiler made from gun barrels. In December 1830, the "Best Friend," America's first passenger locomotive, pulled two cars carrying passengers on wooden

Teddy Roosevelt uses a borrowed car on a campaign stop.

benches on a track near Charleston, South Carolina. By 1833, the line covered a distance of 135 miles. It was during that year Andrew Jackson became the first U.S. president to ride a train, making a journey of 12 miles. When President Jackson left office in 1837, there were 1,300 miles of railroad in operation. His successor, President Van Buren (1837-1841), during his year in office signed a bill making every railroad a carrier of the mail. By 1852, direct rail service was opened between New York City and Chicago.

Up until about the Civil War, traveling by rail was far from luxurious, or even comfortable, but it was a bit faster than traveling by horse and carriage. Trainmen and passengers alike rode pretty much in the open. Clothes were subjected to burning cinders from the locomotive's spewing stacks. Sometimes the coaches made of tinder dry wood burst into flames. Then there was the possibility of a train wreck.

One early railroad tragedy happened to a first family. After winning the election in 1852, but before inauguration day (which was on March 4 back then) Franklin Pierce (1853-1857), his wife Jane and 11-year-old son Benjamin were returning to their home in New Hampshire after a January visit to Massachusetts. The train derailed, killing young Benjamin. Franklin and Jane were uninjured but their loss was especially tragic since Benjamin was their last surviving son. Another son died shortly after birth and yet another had died at the age of four from typhus.

President Abraham Lincoln, at one time a lawyer for the Illinois Central Railroad, was a strong backer of railroad expansion in the U.S. In 1862, Lincoln created the United States Military Railway Service as part of the U.S. Army. When the Civil War began, there were 31,246 miles of track with all but 10,000 miles in the North. This gave the North a great advantage. Armies and their weapons were carried by train for the first time during the Civil War.

In 1862, Lincoln signed the Pacific Railroad Act designating the Central Pacific and Union Pacific to build a transcontinental railroad from the Mississippi River to the Pacific Ocean. After six years, on April 28, 1869, the "golden spike" was driven in Promontory, Utah, connecting the tracks of the Union Pacific and Central Pacific, creating the first transcontinental railroad system. Now it was possible for anyone, including the president, to traverse the country without leaving the relative comfort of a railway coach. Of course, the trip took 10 to 12 days provided the weather held out and there were no breakdowns or other problems.

A good example of how Americans viewed the presidency in the 1800s involved a specially built, private railcar that was built for President Abraham Lincoln between 1863 and 1865. The 42-foot long car featured three compartments, a stateroom in the middle with drawing rooms at either end. The car was decorated in walnut and panels of crimson silk. There were light green silk curtains on the windows and furnishings included plush green sofas that converted into beds for overnight trips. Lincoln never used the car while he was alive. President Lincoln, mindful of his public image, was reluctant to appear in such luxurious accommodations after a New York newspaper chastised him for sometimes forgetting his humble past. The car did carry Lincoln one time back to Springfield, Illinois, in April 1865, after he was assassinated. The engine's muffled bell tolled for the entire distance. The government sold the special car after Lincoln's death to a private individual. There would not be another "official" presidential railroad car until late in the Roosevelt administration.

Just because the government did not supply U.S. presidents with their own railroad cars, nothing said that the president could not travel in the best luxury of the day. By the 1870s, American railroads had reached their "Golden Age." Ordinary travelers who could afford them enjoyed the comfort and convenience of parlor cars and sleeping cars. The rich, such as railroad moguls, and the powerful, such as the president of the United States, usually traveled in private railway cars that were coupled to the end of regular passenger trains. Since the president had to furnish his own transportation, the chief executive borrowed the private cars belonging to the railroad tycoons.

These cars were often rolling palaces. One example was the "Maryland" built in 1872 for the president of the Baltimore and Ohio Railroad, John Garrett. The "Maryland" was "borrowed" by Presidents Rutherford B. Hayes (1877-1881), Grover Cleveland (1885-1889), Benjamin Harrison (1889-1893), and William McKinley (1897-1901). Grover Cleveland used the coach for his honeymoon after he, as a 48-year-old bachelor, wed the 21-year-old Frances Folsom in June 1886.

While looking like most railroad coaches from the outside, the light yellow car was quite elegant inside. The 51-foot-long car had four separate compartments that included a parlor with an elegant sofa, a marble-topped walnut table, four easy chairs and mirrors on the walls. The other compartments included a stateroom, sleeping room and a room for the porter. It was fitted with three rear windows that allowed a good view of the scenery just past.

Franklin D. Roosevelt (1933-1945) would be the first president to have a railroad car dedicated completely to his personal use. The Secret Service decided it necessary because of the dangers of World War II. So in 1942 a special car was designed for maximum security. FDR's railcar, titled the "Ferdinand Magellan," was one of six cars built by the Pullman Company in 1928 that were rented out. While comfortable, the "Magellan" was far from luxurious. There was a dining room with accommodations for 10, an observation room and four bedrooms.

President Benjamin Harrison shown on the observation platform of a railroad coach on the South Wabash Railroad. (Sangamon Valley Collection - Lincoln Library)

The car's biggest asset was the protection it provided the president. For instance, the "Magellan's" steel roof, side panels and ends were replaced by heavy armor plating. The bottom of the car was protected by a metal shield. All this was supposedly sufficient to protect the car's occupants from hand grenades and small bombs as well as bullets. The windows were fitted with three-inch thick, green-tinted bulletproof glass that could stop a bullet fired at point-blank range. When finished, the "Magellan" weighed over 14 tons empty. The armor-plated rear door alone weighed nearly a ton.

President Roosevelt spent considerable time aboard the "Magellan" mainly because most of the 60,000 miles traveled were at speeds below 30 mph. The train could travel much faster, but because of FDR's disability and deteriorating physical condition, faster speeds caused him

The ever-effervescent Franklin Roosevelt waving to the crowd at a whistlestop in Deer Lodge, Montana, during his 1932 campaign for the presidency. (Roosevelt Library)

great pain especially when the train went around curves at higher speeds. One cross-continent trip from Washington to San Diego, California, took five days. FDR enjoyed the slow pace, using the time to catch up on his reading, and perhaps even more important, contemplating the world's then serious problems. Roosevelt, who loved both geography and local history-- especially concerning rural areas--spent some of the time looking out the window and following the route on a road map by his side.

After Roosevelt's death, President Truman used the "Magellan" for long distance trips. Truman liked to travel faster, indeed much faster, than his predecessor. For instance, once he looked up from a speech he was writing at the speedometer mounted on the wall of his compartment. The train was hitting 105 mph! He calmly instructed a member of the staff to tell the engineer to slow down to a more reasonable 80 mph. Truman rightfully was a bit concerned about the disaster that probably would have occurred if the train had to stop suddenly with the 285,000 pound "Magellan" at the tail end of the 17-car train.

President Roosevelt about to leave his special railcar. Note the special ramp that allowed FDR to "walk" without assistance. (Little White House Historic Site, Georgia)

HITTING THE CAMPAIGN TRAIL

Like virtually everything else about the presidency, campaigning for the job has changed dramatically since the early days when it was considered "unpresidential" for a nominee to actively solicit votes, at least openly. Much of the change has come about because of advances in communication, namely radio and television, that has allowed candidates to make their pitches directly to the voters. However, better transportation also made it easier for aspirants to travel greater distances to, make speeches to and shake the hands of more of the nation's population.

Illinois' Stephen A. Douglas, the regular Democratic candidate engaged in a four-way race in 1860, was the first to stump across the country seeking votes. Douglas traveled thousands of miles in the Midwest, South, and the East by train, stage and on horseback. While 1866 was not an election year, President Andrew Johnson was the first president to use a special train for a speechmaking tour.

The railroads that covered the country by the end of the 19th century provided candidates the first opportunity to take their campaigns nationwide. William Jennings Bryan, the Democratic candidate in the 1896 election set a record, at least for the day, by traveling some 20,000 miles by train to meet potential voters in person. On many days he gave more than 30 speeches, most from the train's observation platform. Many were at "whistle stops" where trains would only stop on request. However, the efforts went for naught as the Republican candidate, William McKinley, won the election. Ironically, McKinley did most of his campaigning without leaving his Canton, Ohio, home, conducting what was dubbed a "front porch" campaign since he did not want to leave his beloved wife, Ida, who was too sickly and frail to travel. McKinley did greet some 750,000 potential voters coming in some 300 delegations from his "front porch."

One of the most famous whistle-stop campaigns occurred during the extremely close contest in 1948 between the incumbent, President Harry Truman and the challenger, New York Governor Thomas E. Dewey. President Truman took the campaign directly to the American people, traveling some 36,000 miles in the 35-day trip using a special 17-car "White House" on rails. A communication car chock full of the then latest communications gear--such as a teletype, radio telephone and code transmitter--allowed the president constant contact with not only the White House, but also with key military installations, naval ships at sea and foreign governments. Unfortunately, the press corps accompanying the president had far poorer communications with the "outside" world. Whenever President Truman broke important news, they had to use the local Western Union office to file their stories.

President Truman in an observation car at Union Station in Washington, D.C. upon returning from a campaign swing during his presidential campaign. (Truman Library)

The daily routine usually consisted of about 16 speeches made from the last car's observation platform bedecked with the Presidential Seal. The train would pull into the station while a local band usually played "Hail to the Chief" followed by the "Missouri Waltz," in honor of Harry Truman's home state. The crowd would gather around the rear of the train while a few local dignitaries climbed aboard the platform, often presenting him with a small gift to commemorate the stop. After the speech, in which Truman was sure to mention local supporters, the president would turn around and open the blue velvet curtains behind him, which concealed his wife, Bess, and his daughter, Margaret, who he affectionately introduced as "The Boss" and "The Boss' Boss," respectively. Then the train would pull out of the station making its way to the next whistle-stop down the line.

By the 1960 election, with then Vice-President Richard Nixon running against Massachusetts Senator John F. Kennedy, travel by airliner was no longer a novelty. Thus Richard Nixon could reasonably fulfill his promise to appear in all 50 states before election day. However, it did require him to travel some 7,170 miles by jet literally in the final hours of the campaign. This capped a whirlwind campaign in which Nixon flew 65,500 miles to make at least one appearance in 188 different cities. In the process, he made about 150 major speeches and too many minor ones to count. His opponent, John Kennedy, used the "Caroline," a twin-engined Convair air transport owned by the Kennedy family, in his campaign travels. The $385,000 plane was leased to JFK for $1.75 per mile.

Conveyances for campaigns were often given names. For instance Dwight Eisenhower called his campaign train the "Look Ahead Neighbor Special" during his 1952 bid for the presidency. The "Lady Bird Special" was used by Lady Bird Johnson for the 16-car train used during her solo whistle stop campaign in the South during her husband's 1964 presidential campaign. Jimmy Carter's campaign plane was nicknamed "Peanut."

PRESIDENTIAL YACHTS

One of the most controversial means of presidential travel was the fleet of yachts maintained for the President of the United States. They were controversial because they symbolized luxury beyond what many people thought should be enjoyed by an American president--after all, they were usually not used to go anywhere. Proponents of the presidential yachts believed they were needed to allow the president a more private repast in a hectic life just like Camp David, Roosevelt's "Little White House" at Warm Springs, Georgia, or Eisenhower's Gettysburg.

President Jimmy Carter (1977-1981), as part of his austerity in government, solved the controversy when he declared the current yacht, the "Sequoia," an unneeded luxury and had it sold off at auction to the highest bidder in 1977.

One of the best known presidential yachts was the "Mayflower," which was put into White House service in 1906 during Theodore Roosevelt's administration and would remain in service until 1929. The "Mayflower," built in 1896 for a wealthy tycoon's pleasure, was bought and converted by the U.S. Navy for duty during the Spanish-American War. Indeed, the "warship" actually saw battle against Spanish warships near Havana, Cuba. President Theodore Roosevelt and his family used the "Mayflower" for many leisurely trips up and down the Potomac River not far from the White House.

Franklin D. Roosevelt, a man of many interests, was an avid sailor and spent many relaxing hours on a small sailboat he borrowed, as well as the then-current presidential yacht, the "Potomac." Besides trips out on Chesapeake Bay or the Potomac River, he occasionally took longer cruises to Florida and the Bahamas.

The "Potomac" was replaced by the "Williamsburg" after World War II. The "Williamsburg," too, had been built for a wealthy yachtsman and was bought by the U.S. Navy for use during World War II. The "Williamsburg" saw escort and patrol duty in the icy waters around Iceland. President Truman especially liked to get away from the Washington scene for a few hours of informal relaxation. Truman was known to have come aboard to sleep around the clock to recharge his batteries before going back to his White House office or the particularly grueling 1948 re-election campaign. On other occasions the Trumans would just bring some friends aboard for an evening's relaxation. The "Williamsburg" was considerably more luxurious compared to previous presidential yachts. For instance it had been fully air-conditioned, a real luxury in the late 1940s and its spacious lounges were comfortable. Truman's longer trips aboard the "Williamsburg" included cruises to Bermuda and the Virgin Islands.

Often presidential yachts were used for official entertaining of foreign VIPs. For instance, Winston Churchill, British Prime Minister Clement Attlee and the President of Mexico were entertained on the "Williamsburg."

President Truman aboard the U.S.S. Williamsburg off Key West. (Truman Library)

The presidential yacht Sequoia had a particularly long and illustrious career. It was first used by President Kennedy. The 110 ton, 104-foot-long wooden craft also saw service during the Johnson, Nixon and Ford administrations before being retired by Jimmy Carter. The "Sequoia" was used for a variety of functions ranging from the Kennedys entertaining the President of Pakistan to providing a dance floor for President Ford's daughter Susan and her teenage friends celebrating the nation's bicentennial in 1976. Queen Elizabeth II of Great Britain once stayed overnight in one of the "Sequoia's" four small staterooms below deck.

Guests on the "Sequoia" often dined in the lavish, formal dining room on the main deck being served on a large table that could seat a dozen, using presidential china, crystal and silverware. The walls of the room were lined with mahogany cabinets and buffets and lit by wall-mounted brass light fixtures. President Richard Nixon (1969-1974) used it for quite serious business, often boarding it at the end of a long day in Washington. He would have a dinner meeting with staff members discussing pressing issues while cruising down the Potomac River. Less serious "work" was conducted from the "Fish Deck" and "Sun Deck" whose names indicated their usual functions.

After President Carter sold the "Sequoia," it was used in Florida as a seagoing marine biology classroom, after briefly being a tourist attraction in South Carolina. Then in 1981, it was purchased and restored to its "original" condition by a group of business men and women who then offered it to President Reagan, who declined the offer. However, a congressional resolution was passed that endorsed the donation of the "Sequoia" to the U.S. Navy in 1988. The donation included an endowment to maintain the yacht so the president could use and enjoy the "Sequoia" at no cost to the U.S. taxpayer.

President Roosevelt with shark he caught off Cocos Island while cruising on the U.S.S. Houston in 1938. (Roosevelt Library)

Before the days of air travel, the president had a fleet of naval ships at the ready for long distance ocean travel, though it was not until Theodore Roosevelt's administration that a sitting president left the country, but not the hemisphere. President Wilson was the first chief executive to visit Europe when he sailed across the Atlantic Ocean to the Paris peace conference in December 1918. With the emergence of the United States as a world power, Franklin Roosevelt made many transatlantic voyages to meet with other world leaders at locations like Casablanca, Tehran, and Yalta. Roosevelt also was the first president to visit South America and Hawaii. Thus President Roosevelt traveled on a variety of U.S. Navy vessels such as the U.S.S. Quincy, U.S.S. Baltimore, U.S.S. Tuscaloosa, U.S.S. Indianapolis, U.S.S. Houston, U.S.S. Moffett and on the British man-of-war, the HMS Prince of Wales. After FDR's death, the U.S.S Augusta carried President Truman to meet with Winston Churchill and Joseph Stalin in Potsdam just before the end of World War II.

President Roosevelt chatting with Britain's Prime Minister aboard the HMS Prince of Wales off the coast of Newfoundland in 1941. (Roosevelt Library)

CHAPTER II

TAFT THROUGH HOOVER

"HORSEPOWER" TAKES ON ENTIRELY NEW MEANING

By the early 1900s, automobiles were already a common sight, at least in the bigger cities and towns around the country. However, the nation's "First Family" was a bit slower to enter the automotive age. Even though McKinley had already broken into the modern era with his first ride in a horseless carriage, it would be another decade before the White House began to stock the garage with the president's own fleet.

President William Taft about to enter the first presidential car assigned to the White House fleet, a huge seven-passenger White Model "M" touring car. (American Automobile Manufacturers Association)

25

President Taft and family out for a ride in a Studebaker touring car (American Automobile Manufacturers Association)

WILLIAM HOWARD TAFT (1909-1913)

William H. Taft, the 27th president, brought some major changes in presidential transport when he entered the White House in 1909. Prior to the Taft administration, there were only horses and carriages in the White House fleet. With a yearly allowance of $25,000 for transportation, another first, the White House officially moved from the horse-and-buggy age to the automotive age.

George H. Robinson, a civilian employee in the Quartermaster Corps, was assigned the prestigious position of presidential chauffeur. Robinson's first task was to buy cars for the premiere White House fleet. With a budget of $12,000 and no instructions from President-elect Taft as to marque or model, Robinson went car shopping. The first car purchased was a big, seven-passenger White Model "M" touring car. The steamer came from the White Sewing Machine Company in Cleveland, Ohio. Unlike today when the president's car is highly modified with security and communication gear, the only distinguishing feature on President Taft's first car was the U.S. coat of arms painted on the doors. Indeed, according to a White House executive, the president's White had the "special features which are found in every White car ... there is no way which we can make it better than the car which you, or anyone else, can purchase from us."

White marketed replicas of the "official" presidential car in the form of the Model M-M, touting it as having been built in the "Presidential Pattern." The 40-horsepower Model M-M was a huge car, with a 122-inch wheelbase, and an equally enormous price tag of around $5,000. While the Taft car was an open touring car, a winter top could be installed to protect the president from the elements. The White Company set up a district branch office in Washington D.C., even though in 1911 there were probably only two other Whites in town.

Like a much later President Ronald Reagan who had the engines on his helicopter revved up when he didn't want to answer reporters' questions, Taft used his transport to foil the press. When Taft wanted to avoid photographers, he had chauffeur Robinson press a foot-operated valve that released a steam cloud to engulf the car, preventing cameramen from getting their shots.

Quite appropriately, President Taft used a 1910 Springfield touring car while visiting Abraham Lincoln's home in Springfield, Illinois, in 1911. Naturally, the car was built in Springfield. (Sangamon Valley Collection Lincoln Library)

Like other presidents, Taft took his car with him when he traveled around the country and when he campaigned for re-election in 1912. The car was transported by rail, or when stumping in towns along the Mississippi River, by boat. On other occasions, Taft used cars borrowed from members of the local community. Photographs from the period show the portly Taft riding in the rear seats, for example, of Oldsmobile, Studebaker, Rambler, or Springfield touring cars.

In the early days of the automobile, steam, electricity and gasoline were still in close contention--so it was not surprising that the first White House fleet contained all three. In addition to the White, Robinson bought two enormous Pierce-Arrow limousines from the Buffalo, New York, automaker. The final purchase was a tiller-steered, Baker Victoria Phaeton electric runabout from Cleveland that would remain in the White House fleet until 1928. All four cars arrived in Washington before Taft's inauguration.

The Baker was the car of choice for First Lady Helen Taft, who received driving lessons from Robinson. Taft earned his Connecticut driver's license in 1913. The Baker electric would go on to be used by First Ladies Mrs. Wilson, Mrs. Harding and Mrs. Coolidge.

With the coming automobile age, the White House stables would require a face lift to keep up with the times. Located on the south lawn, the stables were converted into a garage by a representative of the White Company. The modifications were not that extensive, costing only a few hundred dollars, with the most complicated change involving the addition of a gasoline storage tank. But by 1911, even the new garage would be outdated. The last of the White House horses and carriages, as well as the four new cars, were moved to new and larger quarters at 19th and B Streets. The original stable/garage was then demolished. White House employees would still find a use for the horses and carriages every now and again: carrying the White House housekeeper, Mrs. Jaffray, to market, would be one of their regular duties. She refused to travel by horseless carriage. Indeed, the White House continued to keep horses until about 1928.

By the turn of the century, the automobile industry was becoming one of the largest and most influential industries in America. Auto industry leaders often played either an open or behind-the-scenes role in electing the president. Auto workers represented a tremendous block of votes to be won. And Henry Ford, one of the best-known personalities of the first half of the 20th century, was so critical of the president's foreign policies, he even considered making his own run for the office.

So it is no surprise that the nation's presidents have, through the years, been frequent visitors to automobile factories. Candidates would gladly meet with this powerful section of the electorate, greeting the "bigwigs" and the workers on the assembly line, as well as participating in the obligatory photo session where the press snapped photos of the president behind the wheel of the latest model.

Although not schmoozing for votes at the time since he was already out of office, Taft was the first of the U.S. presidents to visit an automobile factory when in 1915 he toured the worldwide showplace of the modern automobile industry: the Ford plant in Highland Park, Michigan. Not surprisingly, he described it as "wonderful, wonderful." By then, the Highland Park plant had become a major Midwest tourist attraction, and Taft was just one of the 100,000 people to visit it in 1915 to see the construction of brand-new Model Ts.

WOODROW WILSON (1913-1921)

Woodrow Wilson, the 28th president, would be the last president to travel to his inauguration by horse and carriage. In 1913 he and the outgoing William Taft rode in a open barouche pulled by four horses. When Wilson left office in 1921, it was in a Packard Twin Six touring car, with incoming President Harding riding beside him.

President Wilson was the first president to use cars almost exclusively around the Capitol. However, he left the driving to his chauffeur Edward P. "Doc" White. Like many other contemporary Americans, President Wilson got caught up in the new pastime: motoring. The automobile would not only affect his public life, but would have a tremendous impact on his private life as well. Wilson, a man of great character and intellect, did not even own a car when he first arrived at the White House, having resisted what he had considered an unnecessary luxury. He simply hired "hacks" when he traveled during his days as president of Princeton University. State-owned cars were used when he was the governor of New Jersey.

President Wilson riding in a 1919 Cadillac during a World War I victory parade in Boston. (Cadillac)

While campaigning for president, his supporters were more than willing to supply automobiles and sometimes carriages when needed. When he and the first Mrs. Wilson, Ellen Axon Wilson, arrived at the White House, there were still only four cars from the Taft administration in the garage. One of Wilson's first presidential "acts" was to declare the "First Cow" occupying the stable that had been converted to a garage "surplus" and had it promptly evicted.

Like her predecessor, Mrs. Taft, Ellen Wilson took to the Baker electric car, which soon became known as "Mrs. Wilson's Baker electric," though the president also used it for leisurely drives. And as would always be the case, the Secret Service followed close behind in their own vehicle--usually a Cadillac. The electric at 25 mph was fast enough for Wilson, who wanted to enjoy the scenery.

The automobile played a significant role in Wilson's search for a second wife after the first Mrs. Wilson died in August 1914. To help him overcome loneliness after his wife's death, the president plunged himself into his work and into an even greater zest for motoring. He was almost always accompanied by ladies of the White House or Washington community. On one trip, Wilson was accompanied by Edith Bollig Galt. The trip "broke the ice" and a romance blossomed, leading to a wedding a bit later.

Wilson enjoyed his leisurely drives so much, some would even stretch to five or six hours long. Life in Washington was far more simple back then. Wilson often took the new Mrs. Wilson or his daughter with him on his drives. If neither were available, he would usually find other ladies to accompany him. Not only had he become an avid car enthusiast, he relished female companionship--even with those other than his wife.

A meticulous personality, he actually numbered or named his favorite routes--such as the "Number Two Drive" or the "Southern Maryland Ride." The tours were taken exactly the same way each time with no deviations allowed. His favorite trips were through Virginia to the city of Alexandria. When the president's doctor thought Mr. Wilson was lacking sufficient exercise due to his sedentary life behind a desk or riding in a car, he took up horseback riding and purchased a horse who he named Democrat.

While cars were now the main presidential conveyance, horses and carriages were sometimes still used. For instance, during World War I, President and Mrs. Wilson went to church in a horse-drawn victoria carriage as a symbol of the need to conserve energy for the war effort. Wilson also used the victoria when his car was in the shop for repairs.

By 1916, the White House went shopping for a new fleet of cars. During the teens and early-twenties, the most prestigious American marque was not Cadillac, Lincoln, nor Packard, but Pierce-Arrow. Pierce-Arrows became the "Cars of State" until the 1930s when the last of them were replaced by Lincolns and an occasional Packard for backup service. Indeed, every president from Taft through Roosevelt used Pierce-Arrows.

Three new Pierce-Arrows were purchased to replace older Pierce-Arrows in the presidential garage. The new cars consisted of an official limousine for the president, a touring car for personal use by the Wilson family and another touring car for the president's secretary. Yet another new car, bearing a license plate with the letters U.S.S.S., was used by the United States Secret Service.

At the time, Pierce-Arrows included much of the advanced and best automotive technology that was available. The headlights integrated into fenders, a feature debuting in 1913 that made it easy to distinguish a Pierce-Arrow from other marques. An example of excellence of the Buffalo, New York-built cars were the two 1917 Pierce-Arrow Model A4-66 touring cars delivered to the White House in the fall of 1917. These massive cars were powered by huge 823 cid, T-head, in-line, six-cylinder engines. For its size, the engine produced a mere 60 horsepower. Riding on a 147.5-inch wheelbase, these Pierce-Arrows were among the largest cars in production at the time. The mechanical drum brakes, only on the rear wheels, made stopping a bit hairy.

The president's black Pierce-Arrow touring car was replaced by a later model in the summer of 1919; it was turned over to the Secret Service, which used it until 1922. Then it was sold as surplus to an Army officer, Colonel P.J. Hennessy, who used it as a family car into the 1930s, eventually winding up in San Antonio, Texas, when the Colonel was transferred there. In 1934 it was donated to the San Antonio Museum where it was restored and displayed until it was purchased by the Imperial Palace for its auto collection in 1994.

Wilson must have liked the Pierce-Arrows, since he bought the 1916 Model 48 vestibule sedan from the government and took it home with him when he left office. He used the right-hand drive Pierce-Arrow until his death in February 1924. This car is on display at the Woodrow Wilson Birthplace in Stauton, Virginia.

Incidentally, in 1917, Wilson became the first president to join the Automobile Association of America and displayed the AAA emblem on his Pierce-Arrow. Like so many other Americans, Woodrow Wilson bought a Model T Ford for use at his summer home.

In 1923, some of Wilson's wealthy friends gave him a Rolls-Royce for his birthday. Like all Rolls-Royce of the day, it was custom-built with a high top and wide doors. The black car was personalized with orange trim, a "W.W." monogram on the door and a small tiger on the radiator cap. The colors and the Princeton tiger signified his alma mater, Princeton. The friends "bought American" since Rolls-Royce were made in Springfield, Massachusetts, between 1920 and 1931.

Wilson traveled far more than most of the other earlier U.S. presidents, and much of it was by automobile. After the end of World War I, he traveled rather extensively in Europe. Indeed, Wilson was the first president to cross the Atlantic while in office. Naturally, it was by steamship.

Back then, the president was not a "traveling man" as he is today. Theodore Roosevelt was the first president to leave the United States while in office when he traveled on the U.S.S. Louisiana to inspect the Panama Canal. Highlights of Wilson's European trip were his motor tours to see the sights of Europe, often riding in European luxury cars belonging to European royalty.

The rapidly growing automobile industry, epitomized by automobile pioneer Henry Ford, was starting to appear as a force in the American political arena. Ford, an open pacifist, disagreed with Wilson's war policies and was vocal in his personal views on world peace. When Wilson asked Ford to help finance his reelection bid, an indignant Ford refused. However, Ford did propose a counteroffer. He would send a letter endorsing Wilson to everyone in America who bought a Ford car. A fair deal for both parties: Ford would sell more cars because of his association with the president and Wilson got a no-cost endorsement from a famous and admired American.

Following Taft's lead, President Wilson would become the first president to visit an automobile factory while in office, and again it was the Ford plant in Highland Park, Michigan. On July 10, 1916, he was greeted by some 30,000 Ford workers who were allowed to leave their machines and the assembly line to cheer the president. Expressing Ford's feelings on the war in Europe, huge banners on the walls read "Hats Off to Woodrow Wilson, the President that Kept Us Out of the War." This was 1916!

WARREN GAMALLEL HARDING (1921-1923)

The 29th president is credited with several automotive "firsts." He was the first to ride in a car rather than a carriage for his 1921 inauguration. The car was a Packard Twin Six supplied by the Republican National Committee.

Warren Harding was also the first president who could drive before he entered office. Indeed, he was a seasoned motorist, having driven his 1920 Locomobile touring car between his home in Marion, Ohio, and Washington while a member of the U.S. Senate. While Locomobile originally built steamers, Harding's car was a custom-built gasoline automobile with a six-cylinder, T-head engine that was capable of 65 mph. He brought the Locomobile to the White House, but the Secret Service would not allow him to drive while he was president. When Harding died in office in August 1923, his wife and his possessions, including the Locomobile, returned to Ohio. Prior to the Locomobile, Harding had owned several other cars including a Stevens-Duryea, Cole, and HAL--all marques long forgotten.

Harding was an "RVer" long before the term was coined. He took many camping trips using several specially equipped recreational vehicles, including a 1921 Lincoln Cook car and a 1921 White camp truck. His camping companions included Henry Ford, Harvey Firestone, Thomas Edison and John Burroughs. Ford's personal chef did the cooking. The 1921 Lincoln "kitchen car" or "chuckwagon" was used along with other support vehicles for outings to western states. The specially built "RV" used a 136-inch wheelbase chassis and the custom-built rear section held a complete kitchen and facilities for storing large quantities of food and supplies.

Outgoing President Wilson and incoming President Harding riding in a Packard Twin Six during the 1921 inauguration. (American Automobile Manufacturers Association)

In a small way, the camping trips in the Lincoln began the long White House tradition of Lincolns in the garage--as well as beginning the tradition of Firestone tires on the president's cars. That 1921 Lincoln Cook car is now on display in the Henry Ford Museum.

Today, the president's limousine is typically airlifted to wherever he travels well before he arrives. In earlier days, the president often used cars obtained locally. Therefore, automakers and local car dealerships vied for the publicity of having their latest and most prestigious models seen with the president riding in the back seat. One of the more interesting occasions occurred when President Harding visited Birmingham, Alabama, in October 1921, in observance of the city's 50th anniversary. At the time, Preston Motor Company was building its Premocar, one of the many obscure marques of the day that were mostly sold in the local area and assembled from proprietary parts. The company was able to convince the parade committee that one of its models should be the presidential parade car.

A special Premocar was built for the occasion. Though just a low-priced model powered by a six-cylinder Falls engine, the touring car was outfitted in an attention-getting ivory paint, ivory silk upholstery in the rear and ivory leather up front. After carrying President and Mrs. Harding through the parade and both ways between the railway and their hotel, the car disappeared and its whereabouts was lost forever. By 1923, the Preston Motor Company had disappeared as well.

CALVIN COOLIDGE (1923-1929)

Calvin Coolidge was known as an easy-going Vermonter, and earned the nickname "Cautious Cal." Therefore, it is not surprising that when he drove, he traveled no faster than 16 mph. However, he did not drive himself while in office. At the beginning of the Coolidge administration, the White House fleet consisted exclusively of Pierce-Arrows, plus the now old Baker electric.

Also known for his thriftiness, Coolidge reportedly traded an iron horse and a lawn mower for a new car for the Secret Service. President Coolidge also struck a deal with the Pierce-Arrow Company to lease, rather than buy, five cars for the White House. This started the tradition of auto companies supplying White House cars virtually cost-free.

Both parties benefit from the arrangement; the government saves money while the car companies gain prestige and front-page exposure for their products. Coolidge's Pierce-Arrow was dark blue with a small presidential insignia, an eagle holding an American flag, embossed on either side. A large silver eagle was mounted on the gauge that was on top of the radiator cap and the car wore D.C. license plate number 100. Otherwise, the car was just like any other Pierce-Arrow. Usually the president traveled quite inconspicuously without sirens or flashing lights. On these occasions, the presidential vehicle was followed by a Secret Service car and a press car, and only ambulances and fire engines were allowed to pass it.

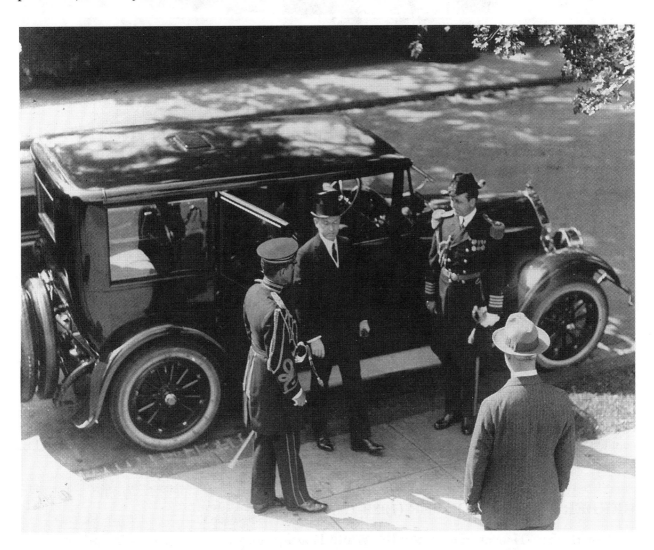

President Calvin Coolidge leaving his 1921 Pierce-Arrow seven-passenger limousine. This photo was taken after Coolidge succeeded President Harding after Harding's death in office in August 1923. Not specially built, anyone with $9,000 could buy a copy. (American Automobile Manufacturer Association)

Outgoing President Calvin Coolidge and incoming President Herbert Hoover riding in the White House's Pierce-Arrow during the latter's 1929 inauguration. (American Automobile Manufacturer Association)

The other Pierce-Arrows included a touring car that wore D.C. license number 101 and was quite appropriate for carrying the president, his chauffeur and four other dignitaries on occasions such as parades. It was used to transport Calvin Coolidge and Herbert Hoover to the latter's inauguration in 1929. The car bearing D.C. 102 was a landaulet used by Mrs. Coolidge, D.C. 103 transported the president's secretary and the Secret Service used D.C. 104. There was even a Pierce-Arrow, D.C. 105, that was reserved for the president's guests.

Coolidge was the first U.S. president to use a Lincoln presidential limousine. It was a 1924 Model L with a sedan body by LeBaron on a 136-inch wheelbase and a 358 cid, 90-horsepower V-8 engine. Some sources say Coolidge was an admirer of Henry Ford and loved Lincolns. President Coolidge reportedly had a number of them available both at the White House and at his summer home in northern Wisconsin. Some more cynical observers of the time may say Coolidge saw Henry Ford as a threat to his political success since the famous automaker indicated he might run for president. When Ford announced his lack of political ambition, the coast was clear for Coolidge to order the 1924 Lincoln, the first of many that would carry U.S. presidents for decades.

HERBERT CLARK HOOVER (1929-1933)

When Herbert Hoover moved into the White House, there were three cars in the fleet that were used by the First Family, Vice-President Curtis and Hoover's sister, Mrs. Ginn.

The "official" White House Car No. 1 was a Packard Model 443, Type 315, seven-passenger "Single Eight Sedan" limousine. By March 1929, it was replaced by another Packard, this time a Model 645, Type 375, seven-passenger "Deluxe Eight Sedan" limousine. In late 1930, a V-16 Cadillac limousine was acquired and used to the end of the Hoover administration. Like Wilson, Hoover bought the Cadillac from the government when he left office.

When Hoover left the White House in 1933, he took a four-month long motoring vacation, traveling some 8,000 miles visiting old friends and sites in the western United States. Presidential auto travel had come a long way from when President McKinley took that first brief ride in 1899.

This impressive 1928 Cadillac town car served during the Coolidge Administration. (Imperial Palace Hotel & Casino)

CHAPTER III

FRANKLIN DELANO ROOSEVELT (1933-1945)

SUNSHINE CARS IN TROUBLED TIMES

Franklin D. Roosevelt, the 32nd president, was the first American president to be instantaneously recognized by most Americans. It could have been because he was in office so long--four terms between 1933 and 1945. Or perhaps it was because, during the Great Depression and World War II, the government became much more involved in the daily lives of Mr. and Mrs. "Average American." Though his policies were often controversial, FDR's love of people, engaging smile and extroverted personality all helped further his popularity.

Radios, by then quite common, brought FDR's voice into homes across America, especially during his famous "Fireside Chats." The rapid proliferation of newspapers and news magazines, especially the ones that presented their stories using photojournalism, carried photos of FDR and his wife Eleanor. A large number of these photographs showed the Roosevelts in the rear seat of an official Cadillac, Lincoln or Packard open-top touring car, or at the wheel of one of their personal cars, also usually a convertible.

THE "SUNSHINE SPECIAL"

The first Presidential car to acquire its own personality and even a name was FDR's "Sunshine Special." Like the First Lady, Eleanor, and the First Dog, Fala, it became almost as recognizable as FDR himself. No one knows for sure how the huge, custom-built, four-door convertible earned the nickname. Initially, it was called "Old 99" in reference to the number originally used on the license plate. Somewhere along the line, most likely in a photo caption, it was dubbed the "Sunshine Special." The name was quite appropriate because the perpetually optimistic Roosevelt liked convertibles and this monstrous touring car was his favorite choice of official transport, especially when the sun was shining.

The "Sunshine Special" was really the first presidential car that was extensively modified before it was put into service. Before that time, presidential vehicles were delivered pretty much stock, except for perhaps the addition of the presidential seal painted on the sides or flags on stanchions up front. In rare cases, the presidential vehicles were treated to some special bodywork.

But beginning with the "Sunshine Special," the Secret Service began to specify the design details of presidential vehicles. Being president was becoming an even more dangerous job. Between 1865 and 1901, three American presidents, Lincoln, Garfield and McKinley, were assassinated and there were several other unsuccessful attempts on the president's life. An attempt on FDR's life in Miami in 1933 probably precipitated the need for much safer presidential vehicles. While FDR remained unharmed, Chicago Mayor Anton Cermak, who was riding next to President Roosevelt in the back seat, was killed.

Incidentally, early in the Roosevelt administration, the Secret Service "borrowed" a 1931 Cadillac sedan from the Treasury Department. This custom-built armored car with bulletproof windows had a rather infamous past. The previous owner was a "furniture dealer" by the name

36

The "Sunshine Special" with its top erected. (Ford Motor Company)

The famous "Sunshine Special" used by Presidents Roosevelt, Truman and Eisenhower. By the time this photo was taken, the 1939 Lincoln model K had received a major face lift featuring 1942 front grille and sheet metal. (U.S. Secret Service)

of Alphonse "Al" Capone. The Treasury Department acquired the car when the Chicago gangster was arrested for tax evasion. It was not long before the Secret Service decided that this car was probably not appropriate for transporting the President of the United States.

The "Sunshine Special" began its life as a 1939 Lincoln Special K, serial number K9655. The commercial chassis, reportedly the last one to use a special 160-inch wheelbase, was sent by the Ford Motor Company to specialty coachbuilder, Brunn & Company, Inc. in Buffalo, New York. Brunn finished the car borrowing little from other designs and using custom parts almost exclusively. For instance, the covers on the twin side-mounted spare tires were unlike any used on a Lincoln before. The finished car was delivered to the White House on December 1, 1939. The total cost of the original car was $8,348.74, including $4,950 for Brunn's coachbuilding contribution.

The order for the car, placed through the Ford branch office in Alexandria in September 1937, included some five pages of detailed specifications. The specifications called for such features as inside storage compartments, extra-wide runningboards, step plates at the rear for Secret Service agents and a heavy-duty suspension. Incidentally, a second 1939 Lincoln was acquired at the same time, but this car, with far less character, was greatly outshadowed by the "Sunshine Special" and thus it and its history was lost long ago.

Most photos of the "Sunshine Special" show it with the top down, but with bulletproof windows in the up position. However, all the windows could be lowered so they were flush with the window sills and the twin B pillar window panels could be removed for complete open-air driving. All windows could be raised instantaneously with the push of a single button. While the bullet-resistant windows could theoretically protect the president from a bullet, the car was not originally armor-plated.

A well-designed folding mechanism compressed the huge canvas top into a reasonably compact package that was then covered by a full boot cover. Initially, the erected top had a bit of extra headroom for the disabled president. However, in 1941, the top height was reduced a tad as a concession to a desire to keep pace with prevailing styling.

Early in his adult life FDR was stricken with polio, losing the use of both of his legs. Interestingly, back in those days, the press treated the president with a bit more respect than he receives today. Only one or two photos were ever published showing him in a wheelchair, though he needed one constantly to get around. Usually, he was shown standing erect, tall and confident. For example, at many speaking engagements, a ramp was erected so his car could be driven right up next to the microphones on the platform. Then, while inconspicuously supported by his son or military aide, he would leave the car and take a few "steps" to the microphone.

Shortly after the Japanese attack on Pearl Harbor, the Lincoln phaeton was returned to Dearborn for a complete renovation and update aimed at providing even more protection during these uncertain and dangerous times. Recycling the 1939 chassis was quite logical since Lincoln stopped building the K-series, a favorite of the coachbuilders in 1939. It should also be noted that there is some conjecture that a K-chassis or two might qualify as 1940 models. The rework was now done by Ford since Brunn & Company had gone out of business. Reportedly the redo cost Lincoln at least $30,000. The "Sunshine Special" was leased from Ford for a token amount.

The car was completely disassembled for a "ground-up" restoration. During the reassembly, heavy armor plates were installed in most panels and one-inch thick bulletproof glass was used throughout. Reportedly, the bulletproof windows and body armor could have stopped a 50-caliber machine gun bullet fired at point-blank range. The huge 17-inch truck-type wheels were shod with bulletproof, metal-sheathed tires fitted with self-sealing inner tubes. Other features included a two-way radio, a compartment for firearms including submachine guns, a siren and red warning lights. The black car was probably given its brown, natural leather interior at this time, as well.

During the renovation, the styling was updated by adding 1942 Lincoln front end sheet metal, grille, trim and bumper. By updating the styling, Ford could obtain worldwide publicity for the new-for-1942 front end treatment, without giving the president a whole new car. New front fenders with pods large enough to house the 1942-style headlights were formed from the original fenders. Because the 1939 hood line was substantially higher than that of the 1942, a taller grille was needed. This was achieved by adding two bars to both the top and bottom sections of the regular 1942 grille. The 1939-style side-opening hood was retained instead of the alligator hood that was in use on 1942 Lincolns.

FDR's "Sunshine Special" is undoubtedly the most famous car ever used by an American president. This is the updated "1942" model.

Lincoln Presidential Limousines
1942-1989

1989 Lincoln Town Car

1942 Lincoln
"Sunshine Special"

1950 Lincoln Cosmopolitan
"Bubble Top"

1964 Lincoln Continental

1968 Lincoln Continental

1972 Lincoln Continental

The 258-inch long, 76-inch wide and 72-inch tall car now weighed in at 9,300 pounds. This put a strain on the 414 cid, flathead V-12, nominally rated at 150-horsepower. Stopping ability was equally stressed since the original mechanical brakes were retained from the 1937 version.

When the "Sunshine Special" was renovated, like many used cars, the odometer was turned back. The 38,000 miles belie the true mileage this car had racked up. The "Sunshine Special" saw almost as much of the world as FDR himself. For instance, during World War II, it was shipped along with the president to such historic conference sites as Casablanca, Yalta and Tehran. The "Sunshine Special" was also used by FDR's successor, Harry Truman, until 1950. It was then returned to Dearborn. Ford donated it to the Henry Ford Museum where it remains on permanent display.

A HUGE WHITE HOUSE FLEET

While the "Sunshine Special" got the most press, FDR used many other vehicles during the dozen years he was in office. In addition to the "Sunshine Special," FDR used an armored 1939 Packard Twin-Six convertible sedan before and during World War II. It, too, offered protection against anything up to a 50-caliber machine gun round. There were other Packards in the White House fleet including a phaeton, sedan limousine, convertible sedan, Super Eight touring limousine and Super LeBaron touring limousine. Before the "Sunshine Special" there was a 1937 Lincoln Model K four-door sedan. The Secret Service used Pierce-Arrows for follow-up duties and a 1933 Lincoln KA-series five-passenger phaeton was also acquired for this purpose.

FDR with some foreign machinery, a Renault, used while he visited France in 1919. (FDR Library)

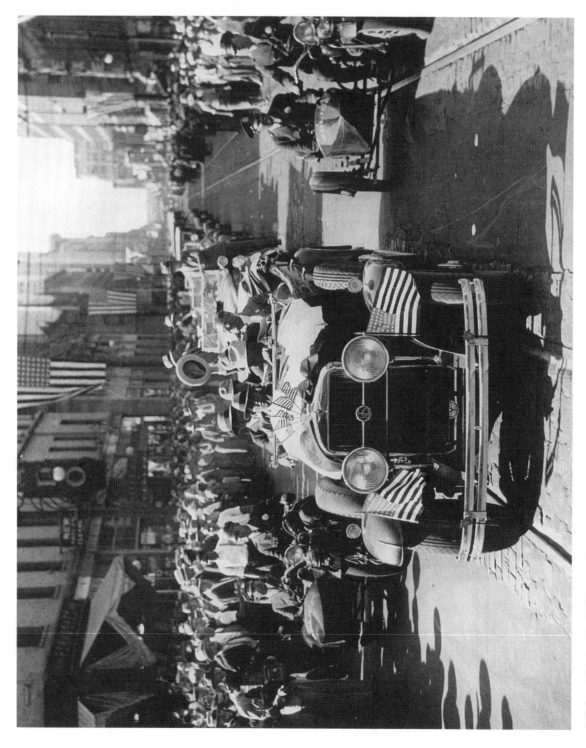

This 1930 Cadillac phaeton was used when FDR campaigned in Denver, Colorado, in September 1932. (UPI - International News).

FDR in a Ninth Series Packard photographed in front of the "Little White House" in Warm Springs, Georgia. (FDR Library)

Two other cars, this time Cadillacs, were often seen in the news, however, usually in the background. In 1938, the Cadillac Motor Car Division delivered two 1938 Cadillac convertible sedans to the United States government. They appeared in the background because these were the follow-up cars that carried Secret Service agents, not the president. Like most vehicles in the presidential fleet, these two cars were given names: "Queen Mary and Queen Elizabeth" after the great British ocean liners that were also making news at the time.

The cars were arsenals on wheels with gun racks, pistol holders and many other compartments for ammunition and other items. They were equipped with red lights, extra loud sirens, smoke screens, two-way radios, heavy-duty generators, runningboards, handles on the sides and rears, plus flag staffs. On the trunk there was an illuminated "POLICE - DO NOT PASS" sign. They were almost always used in parades with their tops down.

The "Queens" were 21-1/2 feet long, had 166-inch wheelbases and each weighed a hefty 7,660 pounds. Three different engines were installed in the cars before they were retired in November 1956. The cars were refreshed at the same time with new leather, paint and tops. The original engines were 431 cid, 185-horsepower Cadillac V-16s, replaced about every 100,000 miles. In 1946, new L-head, 346 cid, 150-horsepower V-8 engines were installed. In 1952, new OHV, 331 cid, 190-horsepower V-8 engines were fitted. The huge cars reportedly could do an honest 100 mph and with the last V-8s installed, the cars could get a decent 14 mpg at a constant 70 mph.

FDR on his way to Annapolis in the spring of 1935 in an Eleventh Series Packard Twelve sport phaeton. (Underwood & Underwood)

Even in safer days of the 1930s, the Secret Service gave the president ample protection. Here the Roosevelts are riding in a 1937 Packard to the wedding of son John A. Roosevelt to Anne Lindsay Clark held in Salem, Massachusetts. (UPI-Acme)

The twin "Queens" stayed in service until 1956, serving not only President Roosevelt, but also Presidents Truman and Eisenhower. They were replaced by two more Cadillac four-door convertible sedans used for follow-up duty. (See entry in Chapter 5.) Reportedly, the Queens Mary and Elizabeth were sold for around $1,500 each by Cadillac, who had leased them to the government. The Queen Mary was purchased by Jack Tallman, a third-generation Cadillac dealer who owned Tallman Cadillac in Decatur, Illinois. The Tallman family has sold Cadillacs since 1908.

Less known than the "Sunshine Special" was a "real" 1942 Lincoln custom limousine that was also used by FDR. It was highly modified and featured a siren, running lights, extra-wide runningboards and grab handles for the Secret Service agents. Like the "Sunshine Special," this closed limousine was returned to Dearborn for updating. After the war, the car was updated and received armor protection. (See entry in Chapter 4.)

While Franklin Roosevelt may have used many cars, he kept Frederick Montford "Monte" Snyder as his chauffeur for most of his career. Snyder, from Rhineback, New York, began driving for FDR after graduating from high school in Hyde Park, New York, in 1928. The time Snyder served as FDR's chauffeur encompassed the period from Roosevelt's stint as the governor of New York until his death in 1945. Snyder also served as the superintendent of the White House garage for a decade.

FDR in Jacksonville, Florida in a Pierce-Arrow. (C.E. Englebecht, FDR Library)

THE ROOSEVELTS LOVED CONVERTIBLES

Franklin D. Roosevelt used many impressive open-top cars while on the campaign trail, beginning with a bright red Maxwell touring car nicknamed "Red Peril" that was rented for FDR's run for the New York senate in 1910. In latter races, Cadillacs, Packards, and Lincolns were usually borrowed from local citizens or car dealers in the cities in which he was visiting. While serving as the governor of New York State, FDR seemed to prefer Packards for official travel.

It seems that both Franklin and Eleanor were great fans of open-air driving. Photos of a smiling FDR, often with the characteristic cigarette holder clenched between his teeth, gave the nation confidence that the disabled president was in good health and able to cope with the enormous problems facing the nation during his many years in office. First, it was domestic concerns as the nation was plagued by the Great Depression. Then it was the weight of the whole world during World War II. Through the years, there were many roadsters and convertibles at the Roosevelt home at Hyde Park, New York, and "Little White House" in Warm Springs, Georgia.

A younger Franklin Roosevelt in Model A roadster at his home in Hyde Park, New York, in 1928. (FDR Library)

While FDR might have used the luxurious Lincoln, Cadillac, Pierce-Arrow and Packard limousines and phaetons for "official" travel, being a president of the "people," the Roosevelts' personal cars were the same brands driven by average Americans, rather than expensive luxury limousines. However, the Roosevelts did have an affinity for convertibles. Through the years, the Roosevelts owned a variety of Fords, Plymouths, DeSotos and even a Willys-Overland. Years after FDR's death. Eleanor even had a neat late-1950s Fiat 1100TV sports roadster, not surprising since her son, Franklin Delano Roosevelt Jr., was a Fiat distributor at the time.

FDR strikes a familiar pose in his 1931 Plymouth convertible at the "Little White House" in Warm Springs, Georgia, in 1933. (World Wide)

FDR in a handsome 1933 DeSoto convertible in the driveway of the White House. (FDR Library)

Eleanor Roosevelt behind the wheel of the 1933 DeSoto convertible. (FDR Library)

President Roosevelt viewing the Norris Geyser Basin at Yellowstone Park from the rear seat of a 1936 Cadillac four-door convertible. The photo was taken in September 1937. (Haynes Inc., Yellowstone Park)

One of several cars equipped with hand controls so the physically-challenged
FDR could drive. This 1936 Ford phaeton was used at his home in Hyde Park,
New York. (UPI Acme)

Being handicapped by polio did not prevent FDR from driving, a recreation he obviously enjoyed. Several of the cars were fitted so he could work the foot pedals with his hands. The first was a 1928 Model A Ford roadster followed by a 1931 Plymouth four-door convertible. A couple of his favorite cars were a 1936 Ford phaeton used at Hyde Park and a somewhat "used" 1938 Ford four-door convertible in Warm Springs. The royal blue 1938 Ford carried Georgia vanity plates F.D.R.1. The car's manual controls included a lever mounted on the left side that FDR operated with his left hand to depress the clutch and the brake pedal. There was also a hand throttle on the steering column, but the gearshift was unmodified. While FDR reportedly helped with the design, the actual construction was done by local craftsmen, often at the dealerships that supplied the cars. After all, the designs were definitely not "high tech," but they did work as intended.

Another specially equipped car for FDR, a 1938 Ford four-door convertible shown in front of the "Little White House" in Warm Springs, Georgia. (Georgia Department of Natural Resources, Division of State Parks & Historic Sites)

One of Roosevelt's favorites was a 1940 Willys convertible that had been a birthday gift from Eleanor's brother, G. Hall Roosevelt. This was an on-off custom since Willys-Overland did not officially offer a convertible in 1940. The Willys was fitted with manual controls and upholstered in red leather.

At either Hyde Park or Warm Springs, FDR was usually followed by Secret Service agents in another larger car. Sometimes, much to the annoyance of the Secret Service, he slipped away without an escort. Apparently, FDR had a bit of a "lead foot" since his cars were often driven at "speed." Many times the right seat was occupied by First Dog Fala. Many of the local residents got to meet and talk to FDR when he drove up in front of their homes.

Hand controls on FDR's 1938 Ford. The lever at left mounted on the floor depressed the clutch and then the brake in sequence. (Little White House Historic Site Georgia Department of Natural Resources, Division of State Parks & Historic Sites)

Another view of the hand controls on the 1938 Ford. The lever on the steering column operated the accelerator pedal. The metal strips attached to the foot pedals allowed the left hand lever to depress the clutch and then "catch" the brake strip to depress it as well. (Little White House Historic Site Georgia Department of Natural Resources, Division of State Parks & Historic Sites)

President Roosevelt behind the wheel of his 1938 Ford four-door convertible talking to reporters. Note the "F.D.R.1" Georgia vanity plates. (Franklin D. Roosevelt Library)

KEEPING UP THE MORALE

Franklin Roosevelt's busy wartime schedule included many trips to support the troops and the workers in the "Arsenal of Democracy." Thus he made several visits to the former auto factories that were now producing tanks and airplanes. During FDR and Eleanor Roosevelt's trip to Ford's Willow Run bomber plant on September 21, 1942, the Roosevelts received a "deafening" welcome from the workers.

The aging Henry Ford--who by now was accustomed to being the center of attention and, to be kind, disliked FDR--was openly resentful of the cheering crowd. Photos of the president in the "Sunshine Special" show a gloomy and even mean-looking Henry Ford seated next to the typically smiling Franklin Roosevelt. Interestingly, years earlier, the Roosevelts were apparently held in higher regard by Henry Ford. When Ford built its 20 millionth Ford, it put the 1931 Model A four-door sedan on a nationwide tour that included a stop in New York where then Governor Roosevelt and wife, Eleanor, took the car for a short spin.

Eleanor Roosevelt driving a Fiat 1100 TV (Touring Veloce) given to her by son and Fiat distributor, Franklin Delano Roosevelt, Jr. (FDR Library)

CHAPTER IV

HARRY S. TRUMAN (1945-1953)

THE "TRUMAN LINCOLNS" WERE "MASS" PRODUCED

Roosevelt's death in 1945 brought Harry S. Truman not only into the Oval Office, but also into everyday use of the "Sunshine Special." The now famous car would continue to be the official White House vehicle until 1950. It was then retired for the same reason many families trade in old models for new ones--it just looked old-fashioned. This "used" car would go on to become a feature attraction at the Henry Ford Museum. Like FDR, President Truman took the "Sunshine Special" with him on important trips. For instance, it was flown to Germany when President Truman participated in the famous Potsdam debates with Winston Churchill and Joseph Stalin.

A 1942 LINCOLN BECOMES A 1946 LINCOLN

Through the years, the White House--or more likely the Ford Motor Company--wanted the president to be seen in the latest models. Sometimes this was achieved simply by updating older cars with later-model styling cues--at least giving the impression they were the latest model. For instance, the 1939 "Sunshine Special" became a quasi-1942 "Sunshine Special."

This 1946 presidential limousine was really a 1942 model with a front end change. (Ford Motor Company)

Another lesser-known example was a highly modified 1942 Lincoln limousine that was used by both Roosevelt and Truman. Originally the car was not armored, but armor plating and bulletproofing would be installed soon after World War II ended. The car was also updated with 1946 trim at the same time. This was quite easy since, like most American automobiles immediately after World War II, the 1946-1948 Lincolns were warmed-over prewar models updated via minor trim changes.

The new version of the presidential Lincoln sported a 1946 grille, bumper, hood ornament and hubcaps. The update was quite logical since the Lincoln custom seven-passenger sedan and limousine did not return after the war. Interestingly, the car could be identified as either a 1942 or 1946 but did not have the push-button door openers that were featured on both the 1942 and 1946 Lincolns. Instead it used conventional handles like the ones used on 1947 and 1948 Lincolns.

Another difference on the modified car was the lack of front-vent windows. The car also lost its rear and external runningboards, but the chrome grab handles on the A-pillars were kept in place. The rear fender skirts were also removed. The large siren with built-in red light and the step plates on the rear bumper were all retained. The car acquired a flag holder in front of the left headlight, multiple antennae and heavy-duty multi-piece wheels fitted with 7.50x15 commercial blackwall tires. Finally, the suspension was beefed up to handle the added weight of the armor plating and bulletproof windows.

LINCOLNS FAVORED BY THE TRUMAN ADMINISTRATION

During a good portion of the Truman administration, General Motors products were conspicuously absent from the White House garage. The reason can be traced to the 1948 presidential campaign when the Secret Service asked Ford and General Motors both to furnish cars for President Truman's campaign trips to various U.S. cities. Ford was asked to cover the western states while GM would take the east. Ford said yes, but the "General" declined. Consequently, Ford would supply all the cars nationwide. Lincoln's all-new for 1949 Cosmopolitans got especially good press coverage when Mr. Truman was photographed on several occasions riding in the rear seat of the flagship, the Cosmopolitan convertible.

President Truman at the wheel of a 1942 Buick convertible during a vacation in Key West, Florida, in 1946. This was before GM products fell out of favor with Harry Truman. (U.S. Navy Photo - Courtesy Harry S. Truman Library)

A bit later, but still before the 1948 election, the White House reportedly asked a major GM dealer in Miami to help supply cars for a planned, post-election Truman vacation to Key West, Florida. Apparently the dealer declined because, like many other Americans, he felt that Mr. Truman did not stand a chance of being re-elected. There was no point, he felt, in supplying cars to a lame-duck president. The White House representative pointed out that, even if he lost the election, Truman would still be the president of the United States until January--but the dealer could still not be persuaded. So the White House turned to Lincoln-Mercury, and finally the answer was yes. Ford, Mercury, and Lincoln dealers in several larger Florida cities arranged to send a few of their better cars to Key West for the November visit.

Four Lincoln Cosmopolitans at the "Little White House" in Key West, Florida, ready to transport the president and his party during another vacation in spring 1950. Also shown are the four Navy drivers. (U.S. Navy Photo - Courtesy Harry S. Truman Library)

This snub by General Motors did not set well with Mr. Truman, who had a perfect memory when it came to affronts to him or members of his family. After his re-election, he told his aide, John Steelman, to have all GM products removed from the White House garage. Reportedly, Steelman's first call when he got back to Washington was to the supervisor of the White House garage. He told the man-in-charge to get all the GM cars off the premises within the hour. The supervisor called back soon after to say the job was completed.

As expected, Ford was asked to supply 35 Lincoln and Mercury convertibles for the 1949 inauguration. The President and Vice-President Alben W. Barkley rode in an essentially stock 1949 Lincoln Cosmopolitan two-door convertible. The car was given the designation "4-X" by the Secret Service, which installed runningboards on the car sometime after the inauguration, most likely in late 1949. This allowed the 4-X to perform parade car duties until there was a replacement for the "Sunshine Special." Apparently the Secret Service liked the car so well that it kept the 1949 convertible until around 1961.

Some may wonder why the "Sunshine Special" was not used for the inauguration ceremonies. The most logical reason, and the one given when the famous convertible was retired in 1950, was that its appearance was far too dated.

Top-hatted President Truman waving at the crowd from the Lincoln Cosmopolitan convertible code-named 4-X during his 1949 inauguration. (Courtesy Harry S. Truman Library)

THE "TRUMAN LINCOLNS"

Sometime after the inauguration, a deal was struck whereby Ford would supply nine new Lincoln limousines and one four-door Lincoln convertible for the White House fleet. A rather loose agreement, arranged by phone and letter, resulted in the cars being leased to the government with Ford retaining title to the cars. Ford was also responsible for their maintenance, parts and tires--sometimes even being asked to repair a dented fender. The ten cars cost Ford nearly $500,000 with the four-door convertible costing the greatest amount.

Since Lincoln did not offer a limousine after World War II, the seven-passenger presidential cars had to be specially built beginning with the new 1949 Lincoln Cosmopolitan. Compared with other presidential vehicles before and after, the 1949 and 1950 "Truman Lincolns" were "mass" produced. In all, a total of 19 were built--including 18 closed limousines and the single four-door convertible presidential parade car. Ten cars were registered as 1949 models, while the rest were 1950s.

Not all 19 were leased to the White House. One car was sold directly to the government of Israel and six of the 1950s were "company" cars that were not leased to the White House, but kept in locations such as New York, Chicago, San Francisco and Los Angeles for use by Ford VIPs. They were also available for transporting high-level government officials including the president, if requested.

All 19 were built on a "stretched" chassis that was achieved by extending the Cosmopolitan's wheelbase from 125 inches to 145 inches. The "stretch" required a beefed up frame and springs. Stretching gave the cars a seven-passenger capacity when twin, forward-facing jump seats were used. But with five people seated in the rear, the accommodations could be somewhat cramped.

In reality, the cars were not that large. For instance, huge 1958-1960 Lincolns sold to the general public were only about a foot and a half shorter. While designed by Lincoln-Mercury Division engineers under the direction of Harold T. Youngren, Ford's Vice-President for Engineering, the actual construction was farmed out to independent coachbuilders. The 18 closed cars were constructed by Henney Motor Company of Freeport, Illinois--a longtime builder of ambulances, hearses and other special-bodied vehicles, usually built on Packard chassis.

The single convertible was fabricated by Dietrich Creative Industries, Inc., in Grand Rapids, Michigan. Raymond Dietrich was probably best known for his classic, custom coachwork designed for the Hollywood crowd. The first closed limousine, designated as Number 100 and used as President Truman's official vehicle, was delivered to the White House in February 1950.

While waiting for the first new Lincoln, the White House leased a Packard limousine for only $500 per year. Number 100, like all the closed cars, was 20 feet long and had a curb weight of 6,163 pounds. While retaining the appearance of the Cosmopolitan Sport Sedan, the cars were all designed with sufficient headroom for the high silk hats that were still in vogue for formal state functions. The higher crowned landau top was covered with a pyroxlin, grain-coated fabric. All cars were painted black.

Power came from a standard 152-horsepower, 336.7 cid, flathead V-8 engine available in all 1949-1951 Lincolns. They were equipped with a heavy-duty Cadillac commercial-type Hydramatic automatic transmission. Between 1949 and 1954, Lincoln, like several other non-GM automakers, purchased automatic transmissions from General Motors. The Secret Service drivers must have found the automatic transmission a real pleasure compared to the massive and undoubtedly stiff floor-mounted stickshift used in the "Sunshine Special." The cars' extended length required a special two-section driveshaft.

None of the cars were originally armored. In the quieter times after World War II, armoring of presidential vehicles was thought unnecessary. However, an event on November 1, 1950, would change things. When Puerto Rican terrorists shot at President Truman at the Blair House, Number 100 was sent to Hess and Eisenhardt for the addition of armor plating, using techniques developed by the Naval Research Laboratory. While never "officially" disclosed, the engine compartment, hood and body sides were probably armored. The car was also fitted with bulletproof glass.

The weight of the car increased substantially over the original 6,163 pounds--about 1,700 pounds more than a stock Lincoln Cosmopolitan sedan. The car was fitted with a type of run-flat tire with a metal innertube that looked somewhat like the wheels on the lunar vehicle used by the Apollo astronauts. Number 100 had runningboards seven feet long and nine-and-one-

One of the 18 specially built Lincoln Cosmopolitan limousines supplied by the Ford Motor Company during the Truman administration. This 1950 model is now on display in the Truman Library in Independence, Missouri. (Courtesy Harry S. Truman Library)

half inches wide for the Secret Service agents. Since the car now had an overall width of seven feet, five-and-one-half inches, red running lights were added to the runningboards. The runningboards were eventually removed when the car had trouble moving through the narrow entrances of some Washington buildings.

All the "Truman Lincolns," including the convertible, were equipped with twin fresh heaters. One was in the normal location under the hood to heat the driver's compartment. The second heater was located in the trunk with coolant tubes running up to the radiator, with an air inlet protruding from the top of the trunk lid. The cars had standard radios in both compartments. An intercom provided communication between the two compartments when the electrically controlled partition separating them was in place. The Secret Service also installed shortwave radios in some of the cars.

Other features of Number 100 included its lavishly upholstered interior, done in a rich gray shadow-stripe broadcloth with gray grain garnish moldings. Originally Number 100, and the three other cars intended for important dignitaries (designated cars 102, 103, and 109), all had gold-plated features in the passenger compartment. All interior hardware and trim, including the door-sill plates, were gold-plated. The down-to-earth Harry Truman thought the gold-plated items were a bit too much, so he had them replaced with regular chrome from car 106.

The VIP cars had special brown lizard-skin cases recessed into the sides of the compartment, including vanity cases, coffee and water thermos flask cases, a writing desk-pad set with a gold pen and pencil, plus cigar and cigarette humidor cases and cigarette cases in

(Upper) A newsman poses in the back seat of the No. 100, President Truman's 1949 Lincoln limousine, trying out the microphone for the communication system. (Lower) The trunk of No. 100 carries a covered spare tire. The duct on the left is for the heating system.

the armrests. The four VIP cars were also equipped with lap robes made of fine broadcloth with a plush lining in harmonizing colors. Number 102 was assigned to the First Lady, Mrs. Bess Truman whereas daughter, Margaret Truman used Number 103, which also served as a "pool" car for visiting dignitaries. Number 109 was the "back-up" car for the president and was used when Number 100 was out of service--like when the car was being armored. Interestingly, President Truman only rode in Number 100, the parade convertible, and Number 109, the back-up car. When the Trumans traveled together, it was never in Number 102. There is quite a bit of conjecture as to where Number 100 went after it was retired from White House service. The best guess is that it quietly went to a dictator of a country in Central America because of its armor protection.

The No. "1" license plate on this 1949 Lincoln limousine indicates this is the one used by President Truman. (Don Richards Photographic House)

The last of the 1949 cars delivered was the open-top parade car completed by Ray Dietrich, which arrived in Washington in the summer of 1950. The car holds the distinction of being the only seven-passenger convertible with a power-operated top. The convertible was designated USSS, for United States Secret Service. It would not be called the "Bubbletop" until the Eisenhower administration when Ike had the transparent, plexiglass top installed. At the same time, the spare tire was moved from the trunk to a special continental kit fitted to the rear, making the car even longer. This was necessary so the "bubble" could be stored in the trunk when not in use. (See Chapter 5 for more about the "Bubbletop").

Like the president's limousine, Number 100, the USSS had runningboards, but here they were really just small steps behind the rear wheels that could be electrically extended about 11 inches. Hand grips on the rear quarter panels served as supports for the Secret Service agents. Like Number 100, twin red lights were located above the front bumper. Unlike the 18 closed limousines, the USSS had the huge chrome fender side moldings on the rear fenders that matched the ones on the front fenders. This feature would also be used on the 1950 Lincoln Cosmopolitan Capri coupe. There were "Lincoln" logos in script letters located on front fenders, but like the other 18 cars, there was no "Cosmopolitan" logo as used on regular Lincolns of the era.

Another one of the 18 Lincoln Cosmopolitan limousines. (UPI - ACME News-pictures)

The USSS had chrome rather than gold trim in the passenger compartment, but was the lone car in the first group of 1949 models to have leather upholstery. The black car was fitted with genuine cherry-red and black leather upholstery and a tan top. Lights in the front seats illuminated the rear seat occupants. When the president was on board, flags were mounted on the front fenders. These were illuminated, as required, by the spotlights. The car was fitted with convertible-style, chrome-trimmed side glass with chrome-finished B-pillars. The latter folded down into the top of the front seat. The top itself, after moving straight up in scissors fashion, folded down into the rear well that was adapted from the standard Cosmopolitan convertible. The top bows were made of magnesium. The then-popular wide white sidewall tires were 8.20x15 Goodyear Double Eagles. The car weighed in at 6,450 pounds--compared to 4,750 pounds for standard convertibles.

ALL THE TRUMAN CARS

Year	Number	VIN	Description
'49	USSS 9EHS	69379	The Dietrich Convertible
'49	100 9EHS	65387	President Truman's car
'49	102 9EHS	65477	Mrs. Truman's car
'49	103 9EHS	68341	Margaret Truman's and pool car
'49	104 9EHS	69120	Car used by Matt Connelly
'49	105 9EHS	68749	Presidential secretaries' car
'49	106 9EHS	68754	Car assigned to John Steelman
'49	107 9EHS	69281	Car assigned to Bill Hassett
'49	109 9EHS	68537	Back-up car for Truman
'49	Pool 9EHS	69830	General use in Washington
'50	108 50LP	6235	Car assigned to Charles Murphy
'50	State 50LP	6243-H	Used by Dean Acheson/State Dept.
'50	Israeli 50LP	6236-H	Sold to Israeli government
'50	New York 50LP	6239-H	Assigned to Admin. Garage
'50	New York 50LP	6237-H	Kept in Radio City Garage in NYC
'50	New York 50LP	6238-H	Kept in Radio City Garage in NYC
'50	Chicago 50LP	6240-H	Kept in Chicago
'50	San Francisco 50LP	6241-H	Kept in San Francisco
'50	Los Angeles 50LP	6242-H	Kept in Los Angeles

CHAPTER V

DWIGHT DAVID EISENHOWER (1953-1961)

Ike was a Car Guy

Outgoing President Truman and President-Elect Dwight D. Eisenhower rode to the 1953 Inauguration in the 1949 Lincoln USSS four-door convertible. He then led the subsequent Inauguration Day Parade in the latest model Detroit had to offer, one of the 532 limited edition 1953 Cadillac Eldorado convertibles. This car not only introduced the "Eldorado" nameplate, but also was one of the first cars to feature a wraparound windshield, a feature that would appear on virtually every American marque and many foreign ones within a year or so. Apparently, any rife between the White House and General Motors had been at least partially mended by the time the Eisenhower administration took over.

Rear view of 1950 Lincoln parade car.

Outgoing President Harry Truman and incoming President Eisenhower riding in the 1950 USSS Lincoln parade car during DDE's 1953 inauguration. (Eisenhower Library)

President Eisenhower "borrowed" a white 1953 Cadillac Eldorado convertible during his inaugural parade in 1953. (Courtesy Cadillac)

USSS BECOMES THE "BUBBLETOP"

The Truman USSS 1949 Lincoln parade car would serve throughout the Eisenhower administration and would not be retired from front-line duty until well into the Kennedy administration. For instance, it carried Dwight D. Eisenhower and John Kennedy to the latter's inauguration. The car was modified and refurbished a couple of times while Ike was in office. Some of these were "running" changes like the addition of red lights, steps, flag stanchions and so forth.

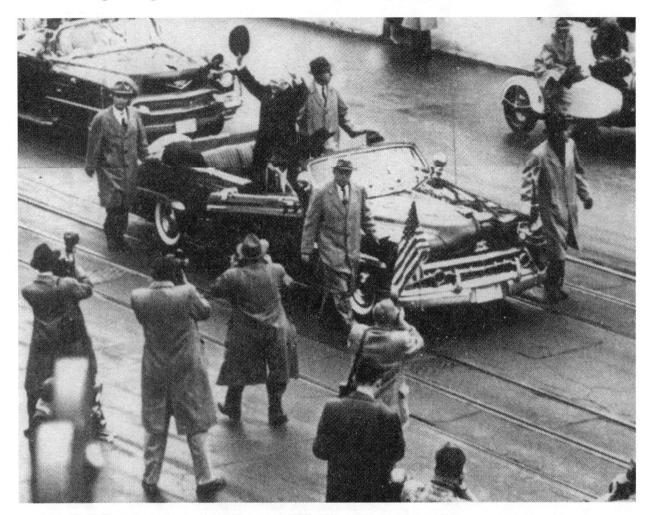

President Eisenhower waves to the crowd on Pennsylvania Avenue from the USSS Lincoln parade car during his 1957 inauguration. (American Automobile Manufacturers Association)

The most noticeable change to the USSS was the bubbletop added at President Eisenhower's request in 1954. The top allowed the public to see President Eisenhower even in bad weather, but still provided virtually no protection from a potential assassin's bullet. The clear plastic top was made of the same material as was used for the clear noses on military bomber aircraft--and it was kept clean with the same cleaner used by the Air Force. The top consisted of four pieces joined by strips of metal. The top covered only the rear section, with a fabric cover over the driver's compartment. The normal-folding convertible top was retained behind the rear seat.

When not in use, the bubbletop was stored in the trunk, fitting in a certain way. Indeed, there was a blueprint in the trunk showing exactly how the top had to be stowed. At the same time, the continental spare tire kit was added because the spare tire no longer fit in the trunk. Sometime in the late 1950s or early 1960s, the tan top with its red bindings was replaced with a black one.

President Eisenhower had the USSS Lincoln parade car equipped with the transparent "bubbletop" in 1954. The top could be stored in the trunk, the reason for the addition of the continental tire kit. As can be seen, the folding fabric top was retained. (Ford Motor Company)

The "bubbletop" could still be used with the "bubbletop" stored in the trunk, thus the reason for the continental tire kit. (Eisenhower Library)

When the 1949 Lincoln parade car finally left the White House, its odometer was about to turn over at the 100,000 mile mark. In addition, it had flown another 50,000 miles so it could be ready at the variety of places the president flew--whether it was Independence, Missouri, or England. On other occasions, when the distances were shorter, it was transported by truck, boat or even driven to the location. One specially notable occasion was when the parade Lincoln accompanied President John Kennedy on his 1963 European tour in which he delivered his now famous *Ich bin ein Berliner* speech at the Berlin wall.

Besides U.S. presidents, the parade Lincoln carried such other contemporary world leaders as England's Queen Elizabeth and Soviet Premier Nikita Khrushchev. After leaving White House duty, it still was used to carry dignitaries. The car would be put to work as a backup vehicle during the Pope's visit to the United States in October 1965. To assure its reliability for the papal visit, Ford invested several thousand dollars replacing coolant and brake hoses and installing new tires.

Just before going on display in the Henry Ford Museum, President Lyndon Johnson used it while campaigning for re-election in October 1964. Sometime before, the car was used by French movie star Bridget Bardot--and Mrs. Edsel B. Ford took it for a spin when it was located in New York City. It was again used by Vice-President Herbert Humphrey during Lyndon Johnson's 1965 Inauguration. The Lincoln limousines located in New York City were stored in the Radio City garage. Interestingly, they were driven by the same uniformed chauffeurs used on Henry Ford's famous camping trips during the Harding administration.

THE EISENHOWER GARAGE

When Dwight Eisenhower entered the White House in 1953, the White House car pool included about 25 cars, including the USSS parade car and several of the 1949 and 1950 Lincoln limousines from the Truman administration. These were now relegated to carrying lessor VIPs. Eventually, several were sold by the Ford Motor Company just as used cars for about $800 each. A few saw duty carrying members of the Ford family. Their prestigious positions as first-line transportation for the First Family were taken by such cars as a 1953 Cadillac Series 75 limousine for Ike and a Chrysler for Mamie.

In 1953, two new Packards were delivered to the White House. These were corporation limousines built by Henney on an extended 149-inch wheelbase. Like the big postwar Packards up to 1955, they were powered by a straight eight cylinder engine. They did not have padded tops like those used on the Derham Formal Sedan.

The White House Packard limousines did have air conditioning, obvious from the airscoops on the rear fenders. As an aside, Packard had pioneered air conditioning in 1940, but dropped it shortly after because the technology was not quite ready. Packard brought back air conditioning in 1953.

While the limousines get the glory, the White House garage had many other cars used for everyday transportation duties. Most were also leased for nominal sums from the automobile manufacturers during the days when presidential limousines were leased. For example, of the 25 cars in the White House fleet in 1953, 14 were brand-new Mercury four-door sedans.

Selling the "ex-presidential" cars provided more prestige than profit for dealers in the Washington area who were awarded the cars after their stint at the White House was finished. A gentlemen's agreement precluded mentioning that a particular car had transported the President of the United States. Thus, as much as they may have wanted to, dealers could not use advertisements like "1953 Packard limousine, custom-built, low-mileage, well-maintained, loaded, and one owner: the President of the United States." That's not to say dealers didn't pass the word around when they had a former White House car for sale--perhaps even providing documentation to verify the origin of the car to increase the car's price a few thousand dollars.

IKE WAS ALSO A CHRYSLER FAN

Like his immediate predecessor, Harry Truman, Eisenhower had a preference for Chrysler products. As an army officer, records show that he had owned a 1940 Chrysler Windsor followed by 1948 and 1950 Chrysler Imperials. Even as president, Ike showed a preference for Chryslers in the White House garage. Apparently, in 1955 there were two Imperial limousines and one sedan. The number increased to three Imperial limousines and one sedan in 1956 and four limousines and one sedan in 1957.

One of the Imperials was a 1955 Crown Imperial limousine. Like all 1955 Chrysler products, the Imperials featured Virgil Exner's all-new "100 Million Dollar Look." In 1955, the Imperial became a separate and distinct marque. Before delivery to the White House, the standard Imperial limousine was sent to famed coachbuilder J.J. Derham of Rosemont, Pennsylvania, for modifications. One of the most obvious modifications was the addition of a sunroof which Ike often used during parades so he could wave to the crowds. The jump seats were removed and the rear seat was moved forward about a foot. Compared to a normal limousine where privacy was important, the president's car allowed people outside a better view of the people inside.

The interior was furnished in tasteful muted-gray cloth with the highest quality deep-pile English Wilton wool carpeting on the floor. In what might be have been a bit of "gilding of the lily," Derham's craftsmen removed the metal framing from the tops of the side windows. Now resembling the windows on the hardtops of the 1950s, they dropped out of sight with just a touch of a button, providing a more open-air appearance. Extra bracing was added to compensate for the rigidity lost when the door tops were removed.

Once at the White House, the Imperial received a few more changes, including flashing red lights hidden behind the bars of the grille and a 110-volt AC generator hidden under the hood to power the car's radio communications system. There was a 140-amp, 12-volt generator that replaced 35- or 40-amp ones used on cars in the 1950s.

Based on a standard Imperial limousine, the presidential version had a 149.5-inch wheelbase. And like all 1955 Imperials, power came from Chrysler's legendary 331.1 cid hemi-head V-8. The engine produced 250-horsepower, quite adequate for a car that weighed around 5,200 pounds. Some of this power was zapped by the somewhat inefficient two-speed Powerflite transmission. Like all Mopars of 1955 with automatic transmissions, the gearshift lever protruded lethally out of the dashboard. The 1955 Imperial used disc brakes that were dropped after 1955 because of cost and complexity.

The 1955 Imperial turned out to be a favorite of Ike and Mamie who used it frequently on trips around Washington and to their farm at Gettysburg, Pennsylvania. After Ike left office in 1961, the car was returned to Chrysler since the five year lease had expired. At that time, the car had been driven less than 45,000 miles and was sold by Chrysler to a private buyer who later sold it to another private collector.

The sunroof on the specially built 1955 Crown Imperial limousine allowed president to be viewed by the crowds. Note the Secret Service was still using the 1938 Cadillac follow-up cars. (Eisenhower Library)

President Eisenhower had the USSS Lincoln parade car equipped with the transparent "bubbletop" in 1954. The top could be stored in the trunk, the reason for the addition of the continental tire kit. As can be seen, folding fabric top was retained. (Ford Motor Company)

NEW QUEEN MARY AND QUEEN ELIZABETH

In many of the photos taken of Eisenhower in a motorcade, the familiar 1938 Cadillac convertibles dubbed the Queens Mary and Elizabeth can be seen in the background, filled with conspicuous Secret Service agents trying to look inconspicuous. Typically, the lead car in a presidential motorcade is an unmarked police car serving as a rolling command post. The president's car follows at four to five car lengths behind. Next are one or two of the follow-up cars. If the motorcade slows to a walking pace, the agents will quickly move from the follow-up vehicle and surround the president's limousine.

In August 1956, the 1938 Queens Mary and Elizabeth follow-up cars were replaced by two more specially built Cadillac four-door convertibles called, quite appropriately, the Queen Mary II and Queen Elizabeth II. The 1956 Cadillac presidential parade cars were 21 feet long and weighed 7,000 pounds. The cars were built by Hess & Eisenhardt, beginning with a Series 56-86 (8680S) commercial chassis characterized by a 158-inch wheelbase and a 365 cid, 305-horsepower V-8 engine. The dark blue cars had beige leather interiors and light beige tops.

The Queens Mary II and Elizabeth II were specially built by Hess & Eisenhardt. They were used primarily as backup cars carrying Secret Service agents rather than the president. (O'Gara-Hess & Eisenhardt)

However, the follow-up Cadillacs were virtually always used with the top down and filled with Secret Service men. The usual complement was two in the front seat, two on the running-boards, two on the rear bumper steps and usually two in the jump seats. Like the cars they replaced, the new follow-up cars were arsenals on wheels with features like pistol holders and a rifle rack. There were also phones and a large extra-loud siren with an oscillating rear light. The car's tires were fitted with a narrow rim inside the tire to support the car should the tires be shot out. The special Cadillacs could travel 115 mph if needed. Secret Service agents were given extensive training in driving these huge cars under all possible emergency conditions, including while under bullet fire or with other agents firing weapons from the moving car.

These twins served not only President Eisenhower, but Presidents Kennedy and Johnson as well. The Queen Mary II was reportedly carrying Secret Service agents directly behind the Kennedy car on the day he was assassinated in Dallas. Vice-President Johnson was riding behind it in a silver, four-door Lincoln convertible.

The Queens Mary II and Elizabeth II were retired in January 1968. The Queen Mary II is now owned by Jack Tallman who also owns the 1938 Queen Mary. The Queen Mary II has about 80,000 miles on the odometer and has been flown all over the world aboard Air Force aircraft. As an aside, another historically important vehicle occupies center stage in the Tallman Cadillac dealership's showroom. It is a 1911 Cadillac that Jack Tallman says "I'm quite certain this was the Cadillac in which Teddy Roosevelt learned to drive."

This interesting 1955 Cadillac limousine was built by Hess & Eisenhardt for Mrs. Eisenhower's use. Most notable was "hardtop" treatment for the rear compartment. (O'Gara-Hess & Eisenhardt)

IKE'S WARTIME CADILLAC

When Eisenhower was running the show in Europe during World War II, he often used a 1942 Cadillac 75 limousine, except of course, when conditions dictated, he used Jeeps, Dodge 4x4s or command cars instead. Like all military vehicles, the stock Cadillac limousine was painted the obligatory olive drab for camouflage purposes.

The only modifications to the car included a red warning light on the left side and a siren. The latter was seldom used because Eisenhower disliked the siren's wail. The car was also used when General of the Army Eisenhower was the Supreme Commander of Allied Forces in Europe, with headquarters in Paris and again in Washington when he became the Army's Chief of Staff. When hostilities ended, the olive drab paint job gave way to a shiny black one. The 1942 Cadillac was finally retired in 1956 with some 200,000 miles on the odometer and 67,000 miles on its third flathead V-8 engine.

The car was auctioned off and purchased anonymously by some of Ike's friends because they knew Eisenhower had become attached to the car since he had spent many hours riding on its back seat. The now worn-out car was shipped back to the Cadillac plant in Detroit for a restoration that brought it back to its original condition--complete with the olive drab paint scheme. In March 1957, the car was presented to President Eisenhower on the steps of the White House. On seeing the car, President Eisenhower remarked that it looked like it was ready for a 50,000 mile journey, and the scratches he had remembered when he last saw the car were gone. The car was then shipped to its new home at the Dwight D. Eisenhower Library in Abilene, Kansas.

When a convertible was not available, General Eisenhower solved the problem by simply riding on the runningboard of this government issue 1938 Cadillac limousine. (Eisenhower Library)

General Eisenhower shows his interest in GM's LeSabre concept. From the license plate and the buildings in the background, it appears it was on tour in Europe.

This 1942 Cadillac Series 75 staff car was used by General Eisenhower during and after World War II. It was later restored and presented to the Eisenhower Library. Mamie Eisenhower looked it over when it was brought to the White House before it was taken to the Library. (Eisenhower Library)

President Eisenhower gets his first look in 12 years at his old Cadillac staff car. Picture was taken in 1957 at the White House. (Eisenhower Library)

THESE IMPERIALS WERE STRICTLY FOR PARADES

If the huge Imperial phaeton, now prominently displayed in the Imperial Palace Auto Collection in Las Vegas, could talk--oh, what tales it could tell. The 1952/1956 Imperial parade car, along with its two almost identical siblings, carried many of the great world leaders as well as many movie stars, astronauts, military leaders, senators, governors, mayors and beauty queens. Four presidents--Eisenhower, Kennedy, Johnson and Nixon--waved at crowds from the spacious rear cockpit. The phaetons have also carried the likes of Winston Churchill, Nikita Khrushchev, Ethiopian Emperor Haile Selassie and astronaut John Glenn.

The parade phaetons were originated by Chrysler chairman, K.T. Keller, in 1951. These were not the first cars Chrysler ever built strictly for parade duties. The first was a massive, six-wheel, 1939 Derham-bodied, custom Imperial touring car. The Imperial was followed by another Derham Imperial phaeton in 1940 and later the famous 1941 Newport dual cowl showcars appeared. Serving as New York City's official parade car, among other duties, the 1940 Chrysler Imperial phaeton carried General Eisenhower during a traditional ticker-tape parade in June 1945, to celebrate Ike's contribution to the World War II victory. The hand-crafted car, made by Derham, was used by New York City for more than 20 years and was finally retired in 1960.

General Eisenhower used the Derham-built 1940 Chrysler Crown Imperial Phaeton for this traditional New York ticker-tape parade on June 19, 1949. (Chrysler Historical Collection)

Dwight Eisenhower using the 1952/1955 Imperial parade car for its intended purpose, parade duty. At this time the car still has the 1952 front end styling. (Chrysler Historical Collection)

Keller's decision for the postwar phaetons was executed by stylists Cliff Voss, chief body engineer Harry Chesebrough, and Virgil Exner, who fathered Chrysler's "Forward Look" of 1955. The 1952 parade cars were built off a Crown Imperial limousine chassis with its wheelbase extended two inches to 147.5 inches. In total, they were over 20 feet long. The car's body panels were handcrafted and completely unique. About the only stock items used were the 1951 Imperial grille and Imperial front and rear bumpers. The clean, unchromed lines and side sculpturing would greatly influence Exner's "100 Million Dollar Look" used on the 1955 Chryslers and DeSotos.

The parade cars were completely open cars, a feature that was only acceptable because of the gentler, less violent times. In true phaeton tradition, there were separate cowls and windshields for the front and rear compartments. Like phaetons of old, there was an abbreviated instrument panel for the rear seat occupants.

The eight-passenger vehicle had two leather-upholstered bench seats and two foldout jump seats stored in the second cowl. The rear doors were of the suicide type and all doors lacked exterior door handles since there were no side windows. In the case of inclement weather, a lightweight Dacron top, stored under the rear-hinged deck lid, could be erected over the rear compartment. However, the driver was left to the elements. This was strictly a "fair weather" car. Reportedly, it cost Chrysler a mere $100,000 to develop the three phaetons.

All three cars were recalled in 1955 for a major update that incorporated many of the features of Exner's "Forward Look" as seen on the 1955-56 Imperials. The entire front end was replaced with 1955 and 1956 sheet metal, bumpers, split grille, Imperial eagle emblems and "Forward Look" insignia. In the rear, tailfinned fenders topped with the controversial gunsight taillights were grafted on. The middle section, doors, and decklid were retained from the 1952 version.

The Imperial parade car as it now is displayed at the Imperial Palace Auto Collection. (Imperial Palace Hotel and Casino)

Cockpit of the Imperial parade car.

A top provided minimal protection, but not for those up front.

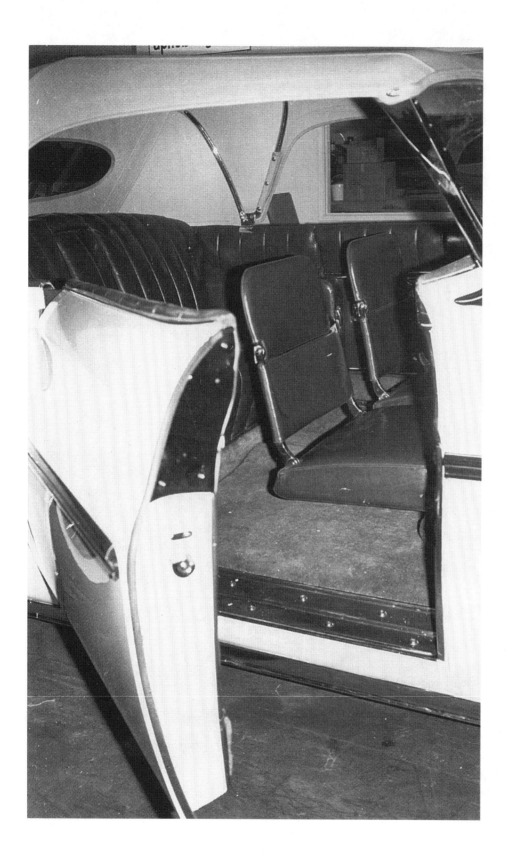

Jump seats for
a couple of pas-
sengers.

Profile of Imperial parade car.

The 1952 versions of the parade cars used Chrysler's legendary 331.1 cid "hemi-head" V-8. With the Firepower V-8's 180 horsepower, the almost three-ton 1952 versions were definitely underpowered. The 1952 versions also used a Fluid-Torque semi-automatic transmission and Chrysler's pioneering Hydraguide power steering. They also used "ahead-of-their-time" Ausco-Lambert disc brakes. A mechanical revamping came with the styling face lift. The cars' anemic performance was greatly enhanced by changes such as a four-barrel carburetor and a compression ratio increase. Depending on the information source, the output was now 235 or 285 horsepower. A Powerflite two-speed fully-automatic transmission was also added, but without the push-button controls used on the 1956 Chrysler products.

The three cars were headquartered strategically in New York, Detroit and Los Angeles. Each was given a distinctively different paint and upholstery scheme. Originally, the "New York" car was black with a light gray interior, for "Detroit" it was metallic green with a natural pigskin interior and for "Los Angeles" it was cream with a red rose interior. After the revamping, the schemes were off-white with red interior (New York), desert sand with red interior (Detroit) and metallic silver with off-white interior (Los Angeles). According to the Imperial Palace Auto Collection, it has the Detroit car.

Even ex-presidents are not immune from car thieves. In 1965, the great general's 1964 Lincoln was broken into while parked in the Tower Apartment's basement garage in Washington. Ike was visiting the Walter Reed Army Hospital. Among the many items taken was the car's 9.00x15 spare tire. The 1964 Lincoln was a far cry from Eisenhower's 1914 electric car in which he and his new bride visited Mrs. Eisenhower's parents.

Mamie Eisenhower behind the wheel of a new 1960 Valiant four-door sedan. (Chrysler Historical Collection)

Dwight Eisenhower recalling earlier days when he drove this 1914 electric vehicle. (Eisenhower Library)

IKE ALSO WAS PILOT

Dwight Eisenhower not only enjoyed driving, but also loved to fly. Unlike other presidents who flew as a passenger, Ike would "legally" take the controls of an airplane. Ike was the first president who had a pilot's license, albeit only a private pilot's license.

Eisenhower was an early advocate of using light aircraft in military roles. Ike's flying experience began in the mid-1930s while serving on General Douglas MacArthur's staff in the Philippines. As they worked to build up the Philippines' security forces, they saw a need for a small "air force" to reach their 90 training camps. Light airplanes that could take off and land on short airstrips were needed to reach the camps, since there was only a primitive road network on the islands.

In 1936 an airfield was informally established outside of Manila. Two instructors were borrowed from the Army Air Corps and a few students were selected for training. Lieutenant Colonel Eisenhower informally joined the group. He was the first to admit "Because I was learning to fly at the age of 46, my reflexes were slower than those of the younger men." Ike got his license in July 1939. By 1941 he had logged more than 600 hours in light airplanes.

In the days just before the war, light aircraft nicknamed "Grasshoppers" were being tested in Army maneuvers in Louisiana. Colonel Eisenhower played an important role in their development when he found a much-needed $24,000 to rent some "Grasshoppers." In those days, the Army usually had to depend on aircraft borrowed from the airplane builders and volunteer pilots for its experiments to see how light aircraft could support ground troops. For instance, Bill Piper loaned a couple of his Piper Cubs and pilots free of charge for experiments at Camp Beaugard, Louisiana.

Throughout the war, Ike, like many other military leaders, used liaison aircraft such as the Piper L-4 and its counterparts to witness the progress of battle firsthand. Even though Ike usually rode in the second seat behind an able pilot, he was fully capable of taking over the controls. By the end of World War II, Ike had ceased flying altogether, except during an occasional long flight on his presidential aircraft, when he would move into the co-pilot's seat and take over the controls to relieve boredom.

General Eisenhower with his pilot, Major T. Walker, in an L-4 Cub during an inspection tour of the battlefield. (Eisenhower Library)

CHAPTER VI

JOHN FITZGERALD KENNEDY (1961-1963)

JFK WAS NOT REALLY A LINCOLN ENTHUSIAST

With all the Lincoln Continentals touted as "Kennedy Lincolns," you may be led to believe that John F. Kennedy was a Lincoln enthusiast. Not so. JFK reportedly was not partial to any brand. Like most members of his generation, JFK received his driver's license on his 16th birthday. Through the years, JFK had owned several brands of cars, including some nice 1950s Packards.

However, since the Ford Motor Company supplied so many cars to the White House fleet at the time--especially Lincolns--Jack Kennedy was often seen riding in, and sometimes even driving, early 1960s Lincoln Continentals. Further adding to the association between Kennedy and Lincoln cars was the widespread notoriety of the 1961 Lincoln Continental parade car in which President Kennedy was riding when he was assassinated.

PRESIDENTIAL CONTINENTAL

The huge, specially built 1961 Lincoln, usually called "The Presidential Continental," is undeniably one of the most famous of all the official vehicles to transport an American president. Indeed, its recognizability was probably only surpassed by Franklin Roosevelt's "Sunshine Special." The navy blue Lincoln limousine received a great deal of press coverage long before that infamous day in November 1963.

Work on a replacement for the 11-year-old "bubbletop" 1950 Lincoln Parade Car started the day before President Kennedy's inauguration on January 20, 1961. JFK would be the third president to use the 1949 Lincoln bubbletop built in the Truman era. Planning for the replacement had actually started about four years earlier. The new car would have more special features and accessories than any other automobile used by an American president. The highly modified car was built by Ford's Advanced Vehicles group and Hess & Eisenhardt, following specifications and instructions set down by the Secret Service.

Now called O'Gara-Hess & Eisenhardt Armoring Company, the Cincinnati-based company is the oldest and largest manufacturer of armored vehicles, with a history dating back to 1876. The company was, and in fact still is, known for its virtually indiscernible vehicle armor systems. It has produced armored vehicles for every president since Harry Truman. The White House open-top limousine project, given the code-name X100, probably resulted from the collaboration between Ford and Hess & Eisenhardt. Here, Hess & Eisenhardt converted 1959-1960 Continental Mark IVs and Vs into limited-edition limousines and Town Cars that were sold to the general public. These specials were not stretched--the 1958-1960 stock Lincolns and Continentals were already large enough.

Hess & Eisenhardt built town cars and limousines off the 1959 Mark IV and 1960 Mark V Continentals. While most went to "ordinary" VIPs, some were specially built for other heads of state such as this 1959 Mark IV for Queen Juliana of the Netherlands. (O'Gara-Hess & Eisenhardt)

One of Hess & Eisenhardt's more interesting projects: This multi-door 1951 Cadillac limousine was produced for King Ibn Saud of Saudi Arabia and his wives. (O'Gara-Hess & Eisenhardt)

Hess & Eisenhardt built this one off, a 1959 Mark IV Continental that was used by Queen Elizabeth and the Duke of Edinburgh during the Royal Tour of Canada in 1959. (O'Gara-Hess & Eisenhardt)

The X100 started out as a stock 1961 Lincoln Continental four-door Model 74A convertible. In stock form, the convertible cost around $7,000 and weighed just over 2.5 tons. When the X100 made its presidential debut in mid-June 1961, some $200,000 had been invested. The car weighed more than 7,800 pounds, making it at the time the second heaviest presidential vehicle after the "Sunshine Special." The 1961 Lincoln convertible was a logical starting point, since it was the only four-door convertible being produced in the United States at the time. The X100 would be leased to the White House for a mere $500 a year. Ford rightfully believed that the payoff was in the fact that the car was a symbol of national prestige and thus had excellent advertising value.

Photograph taken of a 1961 Lincoln Continental convertible, as it is transformed into the X100 presidential parade vehicle. (Henry Ford Museum, Dearborn, Michigan)

The completed X100 presidential parade vehicle without any of its tops before it was sent to the White House. (O'Gara-Hess & Eisenhardt)

To "stretch" the Lincoln, the convertible's unitized body was cut in half and 41 inches were added to its overall length to make it 253.7 inches long. The wheelbase was increased by 33 inches, resulting in a total length of 156 inches. The X100 was also 3.5 inches taller than the normal 1961 Lincoln Continental model, and the ground clearance was increased by two inches.

Half- and quarter-inch steel plates were added to the full length of the rocker panels. Two floor crossmembers and the steel plating were added to the front and rear side rails. The heavy dash panel used reinforced attachments at the side rails. This beefing up resulted in an open-top car that had the structural rigidity of a regular production sedan, and in some areas even more. Hess & Eisenhardt hammered out new body panels using Kirksite dies.

The White House convertible limousine was divided into two compartments, the front one for the driver and a couple of passengers, the back one for the president. The back compartment was separated by a power-operated sliding glass partition and had a back seat that could accommodate three people comfortably--plus two folding jump seats. With the rear roof section removed, the rear seat could be raised hydraulically up to 10.5 inches off the floor so the president would be more visible to the crowd, even when seated. The seats were equipped with foot-rests to provide added comfort. When the president wanted to stand during a parade, a roll bar-like midsection, consisting of a stainless steel handrail, could be used for support.

The most outstanding feature of the car was the unique top, or in reality, its several tops. A variety of top combinations were possible, ranging from a completely closed limousine to a completely open-air convertible when all the roof sections were removed. The formal roof, made of lightweight metal, came in two sections. The front section over the driver's compartment featured a brush-metal finish. The roof section over the rear compartment, which fit from the center pillar rearward, had a black polished covering. In the rear, there was a small, formal rectangular window. This top was crated separately and shipped with the car when it was transported outside of Washington.

The 1961 Lincoln X100 presidential parade car had a variety of tops that allowed the president to ride in complete closed privacy, open visibility without exposure to the elements or completely in the open. In the lower view, the rear seat is in its elevated position. (Ford Motor Company)

A black fabric convertible top came in three sections and was stored in the trunk when not in use. The *pièce-de-résistance* was the transparent plastic top that came in no less than six different panels that were also stored in the trunk. Unlike the transparent "bubbletop" on the previous Lincoln parade car, which was fitted only over the rear seat, the X100's plastic top was transparent for the full length of the passenger compartment to provide virtually unlimited visibility for, and of, the occupants. Since pieces of the different tops could be used interchangeably, many combinations were possible. The tops were built to close tolerances, using special jigs and features.

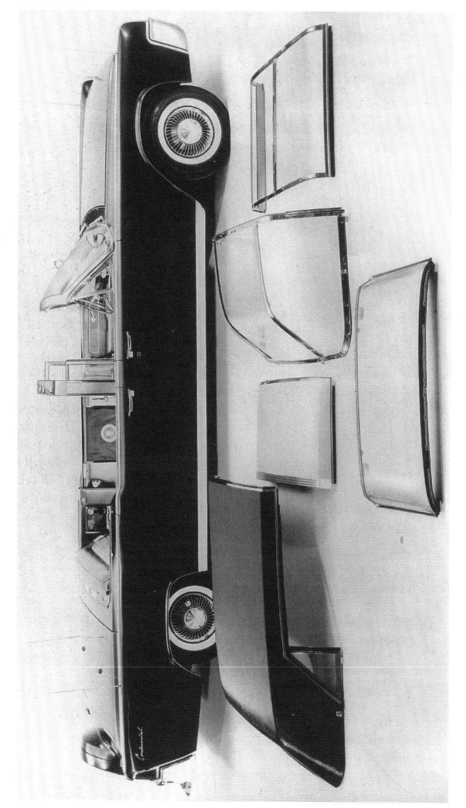

The X100 used an array of roof sections to provide the various roof configurations. (Ford Motor Company)

Front view of the X100. (*Old Cars Weekly*, Krause Publications)

The Continental tire kit was partially recessed into the trunk lid and actually held a spare tire since all the space in the trunk itself was needed for storing the tops. However, it is quite doubtful that one of the car's truck-size 8.90x15 Firestone bullet-resistant tires would ever be changed at the side of the road. Also at the rear were two footstands built into the bumper for Secret Service agents. When used, retractable grip handles were attached to the trunk lid. Two more automatically retractable steps for agents were located on either side of the car. Here, the grab handles were recessed into the body.

The navy blue car had flagstaffs on either front fenders. At night, the flags were illuminated by remote-controlled spotlights. Two flashing lights were recessed into the front bumper guards and there was, of course, the obligatory siren. Incidentally, the navy blue paint was actually a special dark metallic blue, and it was used because it gave the right shiny black appearance at night under the television lighting used during the 1960s.

Inside, the car was upholstered in a combination of light and dark blue leather. The Presidential Seal was prominently embroidered on the two lap robes that were integrated into trim panels on the inside of both rear doors and the floor was carpeted in blue-mouton carpet. Nonglaring interior floodlights illuminated the president at night. Reading lights were located in the rear corners of the metal roof. There were twin two-way radio/telephones, one each in the passenger and driver's compartments.

Other features included separate heating and air conditioning systems for the front and rear compartments. Incidentally, this was the first presidential limousine with complete air conditioning. Other "built-in" accessories included an emergency light, fire extinguisher, automatic trunk lid, first aid kit and special storage compartments. The driver used a master control console with individual switches for the lights and other functions.

The car used the standard 430 cid, 300-horsepower engine. A special fuel pump was added to prevent vapor lock during slow moving parades on hot days. Even though the car weighed considerably more than a regular 1961 Lincoln, according to the Secret Service, the Lincoln "accelerated, stopped and handled remarkably well." Maneuvering the 21-foot car was surprisingly easy because of power steering and a short turning diameter for a car of its size. The car's suspension, springs, axle, and bearings were beefed up using heavy-duty parts. The much longer driveshaft was redesigned and reinforced. Flared aluminum brake drums were used in the front and the rear.

The car was updated a bit in 1962, at which time a 1962-style grille was substituted. The huge Continental Mark II wheel covers were replaced by lighter weight covers of 1956/57 Lincoln design. These were the most recent 15-inch designs in the Lincoln parts bin since the 1958-1960 Lincolns used 14-inch wheels. A few years later, it acquired 1965-type taillights.

All of the car's protective features were for naught since the top panels were left off during that fateful ride in Dallas. It didn't help that Secret Service agents were not riding on the side and rear steps. But, in all fairness, the plexiglass top was not bulletproof and, at best, may have only deflected the bullets. However, a Secret Service agent on the right-hand rear step could have been in the direct line of fire between the Texas School Book Depository Building and the president. The car, as you will see, was extensively modified for much greater protection during the Johnson administration and was used through 1977. (See Chapter 7.)

This Checker is reportedly the taxi hired by Lee Harvey Oswald after assassinating President Kennedy. (Pate Museum of Transportation)

AN INFAMOUS TAXI

The controversy regarding Kennedy's assassin, as well as the many conspiracy theories, will probably persist forever. However, the official and most widely accepted position is that the dastardly deed was performed by Lee Harvey Oswald. There is a car--or rather a Checker taxi, now on display in the Pate Museum of Transportation in Fort Worth, Texas--that played a role on that infamous day. As the story goes, Oswald used the taxi in fleeing the scene of the crime. Apparently, Oswald boarded a city bus, but soon exited when the bus was gridlocked in traffic. He then hailed a Checker taxicab driven by veteran driver Bill Whaley. Whaley drove an uncommunicative Oswald until he snapped, "This is fine, right." The fare was 95 cents. Oswald handed Whaley a dollar bill and left. The Checker taxi and Bill Whaley had their "15 minutes of fame."

Mrs. John F. Kennedy steps from a Cadillac limousine during a state visit with President Kennedy to Ottawa, Ontario, Canada.

JACKIE'S CARS

Several White House cars were reportedly leased solely for the use of Mrs. Kennedy. The first lady used the cars when she performed her regular duties, attending functions at home or abroad without the president--or when, according to protocol requirements, the Kennedys traveled in separate cars. Two cars were dubbed the "First Lady's Car"--not surprising since, during the Kennedy administration, the White House fleet had grown to a total of 131 vehicles.

The first lady's section of the fleet included a 1961 Crown Imperial Ghia limousine, one of only 99 built between 1957 and 1961. The Ghia in the title came from the fact that it was hand-crafted by famed Italian coachbuilder Ghia. Ghia started with a standard LeBaron Imperial sedan that was shipped from Detroit to Genoa, Italy. Here the car was stretched to increase the wheelbase from the standard 129 inches to 149.5 inches. Other features included limousine-type doors that extended into the roof--which reportedly took 17 hours alone to fit on each car. The stepped rear portion of the roof was done in black leather to match the black exterior.

The interior was finished in the highest quality broadcloth, glove-grade milled leather, sheared mouton carpeting and cabinet woods tastefully accented with metal moldings. Jump seats provided eight-passenger seating. The chauffeur compartment used narrow-piped black leather and matching black nylon carpeting that was also used in the luggage compartments. The elegant car was fitting transport for the equally elegant Jacqueline Kennedy. While the car cost $18,500, the White House only leased it.

The second car frequently used by Mrs. Kennedy was a custom-built 1962 Lincoln sedan. It was one of only three Lincoln Continental Town Limousine conversions done by Hess & Eisenhardt. One was assigned to Mrs. Edsel B. Ford and a second for VIP transportation at Ford's public relations office in New York. The third went to the White House where it was given the code number 297-X by the Secret Service.

Although deemed a limousine, it had the same 123-inch wheelbase as the rest of the Lincoln Continentals. While basically a sedan, it had the chassis and underbody of a convertible. It was not armored. The car was called the "small bubbletop" because of the one-piece transparent plastic section over the rear passenger compartment. There was a one-piece black vinyl top that was stored in the trunk, used to provide closed-limousine privacy when needed. The rest of the top, forward of the B-pillar, was vinyl over steel. Of the three cars built, only the White House's 297-X had a bubbletop.

On many occasions, standard Lincoln Continental convertibles, such as this 1962 model, were pressed into presidential parade duty as when JFK visited Illinois in October 1962. Even in stock form, the four-door convertibles seemed right for carrying the president. (Sangamon Valley Collection, Lincoln Library)

Other features included a custom interior with black leather seats in the front compartment. The rear sported a combination of baby blue leather-and-wool fabric plus heavy-cut pile carpet in the rear. Spotlights on the floor were used to illuminate the rear-seat occupants at night. The car was fitted with an intercom system, separate front and rear air conditioning units, twin two-way radio/telephones in the rear, hidden flag stanchions on the front fenders, a siren and special red lights custom built into the front bumper guards. A divider separated the two compartments.

The "small bubbletop" was also used by future First Ladies Lady Bird Johnson and Patricia Nixon. Other dignitaries to ride on the rear seat included Pope Paul VI, Mexican "First Lady" Mrs. Lopez Mateo, President Marcos of the Philippines and the wives of the Apollo 8 astronauts during a 1969 ticker-tape parade in New York City. It was used by President and Mrs. Lyndon Johnson during a 1966 tour to the Far East and during the wedding of Lucy Johnson to Patrick Nugent. The car was retired in 1970 and donated to the Henry Ford Museum in 1972. The Ford Museum subsequently sold it at auction. Since 1985, it has been on display at the Imperial Palace Auto Collection in Las Vegas, Nevada.

The X100 used an array of roof sections to provide the various roof configurations. (Ford Motor Company)

Some details of the 297-X. (Bill Siuru)

Some details of the 297-X. (Bill Siuru)

OTHER "KENNEDY LINCOLNS"

The Kennedys also used Lincoln Continentals while at the Kennedy "compounds" in Hyannisport, Massachusetts, and Palm Beach, Florida. Jackie Kennedy used a Lincoln Continental when she was in New York City. One of these, a 1962 four-door sedan that was used to take the Kennedys to church and Jackie on shopping trips in Florida, has seen a succession of owners since it was disposed of by the Secret Service.

CHAPTER VII

LYNDON BAINES JOHNSON (1963-1969)

LBJ WAS A LINCOLN FAN!

Lyndon Johnson became president upon the sudden death of John Kennedy and inherited the 1961 presidential Lincoln limousine in which JFK was assassinated. Car-wise, one of LBJ's first acts was to have the car flown back from Dallas to Washington. It was stored until President Johnson sent it back to the Ford Motor Company in Dearborn and subsequently back to Hess & Eisenhardt in Cincinnati for a complete revamping. After one month in office, President Johnson also reduced the executive office's fleet of limousines from 131 to a mere 20.

"THE QUICK FIX"

Immediately after Kennedy's assassination, several high level committees and commissions were formed to find out what happened and recommend ways to prevent such a tragedy from occurring again. One group of experts was assembled within two weeks of JFK's assassination to propose changes to the president's official car for greater protection. Six people representing the Secret Service, the Army Materials Research Center at the Watertown Arsenal in New York, Pittsburgh Plate & Glass (PPG), and Hess & Eisenhardt met to come up with concepts.

The group concluded that the best solution was a complete rebuilding of the X100. The project came to be known as "The Quick Fix." Ideas went from the drawing board to the finished product in a mere 13 weeks--at least for the protection equipment. A threat analysis was conducted by the Watertown Arsenal, which came up with three of the most probable ways someone might try to assassinate a president. Most likely, they determined, a would-be assassin would use a weapon such as a rifle, pistol or even a knife--any of which could be concealed. They also concluded that small explosive devices, grenades or small bombs might be used or a poison gas bomb, concealed in a pocket, could be thrown at the president. Modifications to the car would come to reflect these findings.

The redone presidential Continental would not reappear in Washington until June of 1964. Then, for some undisclosed reason, the car redesignated as a 1964 model, would not see presidential duty again until October 1964. On its first outing, it carried President Johnson and President Diosado Macapagal of the Philippines in a short parade in Washington. While the 1961 Parade Lincoln "was in the shop," President Johnson borrowed one of FBI Director J. Edgar Hoover's official cars. Apparently, Hoover kept several cars in major cities around the country. This particular one was a 1961 Cadillac Fleetwood 75 limousine, equipped with security features including bullet-resistant glass and steel plating. Reportedly, it was not the best vehicle in the FBI chief's "fleet."

For many years, the details on the protective features installed during "The Quick Fix" were classified for obvious reasons. Since the car was retired from service, some technical information has been released. After the car left the fleet in 1977, it was donated to the Henry Ford Museum where it remains on display.

Ford and Hess & Eisenhardt made extensive modifications, most of them to heed the recommendations of the several groups that investigated the assassination in minute detail. Incidentally, pieces of the original car--including its interior--were carefully preserved by the Ford Motor Company.

The revamped X100 required a huge expenditure of time and engineering talent. It is estimated that one million dollars was spent on "The Quick Fix," far more than was spent on any previous presidential vehicle. History will record it as one of the most interesting cars ever constructed. Upon completion, the Lincoln weighed 9,500 pounds--about double the initial weight. A custom-designed engine from Ford partially compensated for the additional weight.

Capping the technological advancements was the car's new top that was now permanently fixed to the car. It was made of expensive "water white," bullet-resistant glass sandwiched in up to five layers of polycarbonate and vinyl and varied in thickness from one inch to 1-13/16 inches. This opaque armor provided transparent protection with minimum distortion. The top, including the windshield, was composed of 13 separate pieces. The 1,500-pound rear-roof section was the largest piece of bullet-resistant, cast-curved glass produced up to that time. Produced by Pittsburgh Plate & Glass, this top was a major engineering feat and reportedly cost $125,000 alone! According to the experts, the redone car provided complete immunity from rifle and pistol fire.

The car's new bulletproof windows were made of no less than eight panes of glass. They were reported capable of stopping virtually any type of bullet. In 1967, at President Johnson's request, the fixed right rear door window was converted to a movable pane operated by a heavy-duty power regulator. A sliding glass partition was added between the front and rear compartments. This replaced the metal bar that previously separated the compartments. A black detachable cover could be placed over the rear passenger compartment's glass enclosure for privacy. This matched the black vinyl-clad section on the driver's compartment.

The 1961 presidential limousine was returned to Hess & Eisenhardt in Cincinnati after the Kennedy assassination and rebuilt in this form. Compare this to the "before" shot in Chapter 6 to see the obvious differences. (O'Gara-Hess & Eisenhardt)

The redone 1961/1964 Lincoln parade car ready to transport the president. (U.S. Secret Service)

The principle armor used in other parts of the car was also "high-tech." The 3/8-inch sandwich of titanium steel was produced in limited quantities and "released to federal agencies only." The armor was used strategically in the doors, rear quarter panels, front roof panel, the roof rails and behind the rear seat. Another type of armor, HY-100 steel, designed for protection against blasts from explosives, rather than projectiles like bullets, was used in the floor, rear seat base and rear seat riser. Blast protective floor plates were installed. Rigorous tests at the Army's Aberdeen Proving Ground in Maryland demonstrated that they could withstand a blast from up to eight sticks of dynamite. Steel armor plating alone added 1,600 pounds to the car's weight.

Another technique for ballistic protection was a lightweight and flexible 12-ply fabric armor. This was used in such odd shaped locations as the back of the front seat, the rear doors, center body pillar and rear quarter panels. The grab handles for the agents were now permanently attached to the trunk. Extended steps for Secret Service agents were now located just in front of the rear wheels.

The rear interior was updated with 1964-style biscuit-scheme upholstery. A center armrest and reading lamp were added to the rear compartment. A microphone and speaker was also added so outside noises could be heard through the rear armor and bulletproof windows. Finally, the car was fitted with larger bulletproof tires that were made of rubber-coated aluminum. The bulletproof tires were successfully demonstrated at speeds of up to 100 mph on the Ford test track.

There was a heavy-duty air conditioning system with filters installed to combat all commonly known poison gases. The previous 300-horsepower, 430 cid V-8 was replaced by a hand-built and higher performance 430 cid unit that produced 50 more horsepower. There was a heavier-duty transmission plus beefed-up suspension, axles, brakes and steering. Finally, the previously navy blue car was repainted black.

Lessons learned from "The Quick Fix" were applied in subsequent presidential vehicles albeit with some modifications and most importantly, an infusion of ever more advanced technology. For example, each generation of presidential limousines has offered more protection with less total vehicle weight because of the development of improved, lighter materials.

Rear view of the 1961 Lincoln parade car, now called a 1964 after the major modifications. (Ford Motor Company)

Redone X100, 1961 Lincoln parade car with the vinyl top in place. While it provided privacy, it was not exactly pretty. This photo was taken on July 24, 1970, when President Nixon visited Fargo, North Dakota. (Jim Benjaminson)

TWO NEW FOLLOW-UP CARS

Two unique Lincolns were delivered to the White House fleet in October 1967. While custom-built for Ford, this time by Lehmann-Peterson in Chicago, they were not used to transport the president per se. That is because these were, in Secret Service terminology, "follow-up" vehicles meant to carry agents, medical personnel and so forth. Cars such as the "Sunshine Special" and the 1961/1964 presidential Continental were "parade" cars. The president's caravan often included a "backup," usually an older parade car that could be quickly substituted for the president's limousine, should the parade car break down or an emergency arise. Usually an expert mechanic, also a Secret Service agent wearing the obligatory coat and tie, rode in the "backup" vehicle with his briefcase filled with automotive tools.

The two new Lincoln follow-up cars replaced the pair of 1956 Cadillac Queen Mary II and Queen Elizabeth II convertible sedans. While listed as 1968s, they were really based on the 1967 Lincoln Continental since this was the last year Lincoln offered a four-door convertible. While having 1967-type interiors, they were updated with 1968 cosmetics. Specially designed for Secret Service agents, not dignitaries, they carried many unusual security features such as 11-inch-wide full-length runningboards that ran continuously between the front and rear wheels. There was another full-length 11-inch-wide runningboard at the rear, this one hydraulically retractable and doubling as a rear bumper. There were full-width assist bars that could be retracted hydraulically into the rear deck lid. Agents riding on the side runningboards held onto the chrome assist bars alongside the side windows.

The rear doors were especially interesting in that they were slit vertically down their centers so the forward half could slide over the rear section. This allowed agents on the runningboards the ability to enter the rear compartment through a 15-inch wide walkway. While normally operated with the top down, there was a convertible top for use in inclement weather. The top featured a large transparent, vinyl "skylight" that still allowed agents a good view of any potential dangers from above. There were bucket seats up front with a rear-facing seat filling the center gap. The cars were both fitted with highly advanced communications equipment, public address speakers, siren and red flasher lights.

One of two special-built 1968 Lincoln Continental four-door convertibles that replaced the Queen Mary II and Queen Elizabeth II for follow-up duty. The rear doors of the four-door convertibles were redesigned into two sections to allow Secret Service agents to enter the moving car from the running-boards through a 15 inch wide walk-through. (Ford Motor Company)

Rear view of the 1968 Lincoln Continental four-door convertible with its top installed.

Reportedly, when these cars were placed in service, agents, accustomed to the somewhat sluggish 1956 Cadillac follow-up cars, were a bit startled with the Lincoln's snappy acceleration.

JOHNSON'S CARS REFLECTED HIS PERSONALITY

Lyndon Johnson truly liked cars, especially Lincolns. He kept a fleet of white Lincolns, several Cadillacs of 1950s vintage and a 1934 Ford phaeton at the Johnson Ranch in Texas. There was even a fire truck and an Amphicar. When dignitaries visited the ranch, he liked to take them for a ride in the Amphicar. After driving the car into the Pedernales River, he would claim the brakes failed, and then laugh.

The four-door Lincoln Continentals were favorites of LBJ. Early in his career, a big white Lincoln convertible with a beige interior became a symbol of the Senator from Texas. However, LBJ also owned another impressive vehicle, a 1957 Crown Imperial, while serving as a senator. When Lincoln finally came out with the four-door convertible in 1961, LBJ had found his automobile.

Lyndon Johnson at his Texas ranch with one of his favorite cars, a Lincoln four-door convertible. (Yoichi R. Okamota, Johnson Library)

Probably one of the most unusual cars to be used by a U.S. President. Lyndon Johnson and his Amphicar. (Yoichi R. Okamota, Johnson Library)

While most limousines that carry the president are black or navy blue and quite somber, this was not the case with this 1964 Cadillac Series 75. It offered a definite contrast with its red body and white vinyl top. (Imperial Palace Hotel & Casino)

CHAPTER VIII

RICHARD MILHOUS NIXON (1969-1974)

and GERALD RUDOLPH FORD (1974-1977)

President Nixon had a removable panel added to the 1961/1964 Lincoln Continental parade car so he could have more personal contact with the crowd. (John Conde)

Richard Nixon was the third president to use the 1961/1964 Lincoln Continental parade car built for the Kennedy administration and extensively modified after JFK's assassination. As Dwight Eisenhower's vice-president, Richard Nixon used unmodified Cadillac limousines that were "traded in" just about every year.

President Nixon had a hinged roof panel added in 1969 to allow him to stand in the rear compartment during a slow-moving parade. An open roof would be featured on several future presidential limousines now that security considerations ruled out the possibility of the president riding in a convertible. By using a "sunroof," the president could quickly withdraw behind the bulletproof glass if any trouble should erupt. The 1961/1964 parade car, one of the most famous of all presidential cars, would serve as the nation's "First Car" until it was replaced by another custom-built Lincoln in 1972 and finally retired from service in 1977.

As an aside, it is a bit ironic that Lincolns would play such a major role in transporting the president for so many years. In 1917, Henry M. Leland, the founder of Cadillac, left General Motors to found the Lincoln Motor Company. The first Lincoln appeared in 1920 when Leland was already 75 years old. Leland chose the name Lincoln after Abraham Lincoln, the president Leland had voted for in 1864. Incidentally, this was not the only car brand sharing its name with a U.S. president. These included:

Marque	Years Produced
Cleveland	1902-1906, 1909, and 1919-1926
Grant	1914-1923
Harding	1916
Harrison	1904-1907
Jackson	1903-1923
Madison	1915-1918
Monroe	1914-1924
Roosevelt	1929-1930
Washington	1908-1909, 1911-1923, and 1925

Of these, only the Lincoln survived.

President Nixon in the 1961/1964 Lincoln Continental parade car during a 1970 visit to Fargo, North Dakota. The photo shows how well the car allowed the president to be seen while still allowing maximum protection. (Jim Benjaminson)

111

An overview of some of the presidential limousines used from the late 1930s to the early 1970s--in these four instances, all Lincolns. Top to bottom: The 1968-69 Lincoln Continental parade car showing its unique roof panels; the famous 1961-64 Lincoln presidential limousine after it was completely redone following the assassination of John F. Kennedy; the Lincoln Cosmopolitan parade car used by Harry Truman, which features the "bubble-top" installed during the Eisenhower administration; and, a young car enthusiast gets a close-up look at Franklin Roosevelt's original "Sunshine Special" Lincoln.

"1968 or 1969" PRESIDENTIAL CONTINENTAL

In addition to the twin White House 1968 Lincoln Continental Secret Service "follow-up" vehicles (see Chapter 7) another special presidential Lincoln was constructed during the Johnson administration. However, it was first used by then President-elect Richard Nixon in November 1968 on a trip from the airport to the Walter Reed Army Hospital. Originally the car was based on a 1967 Lincoln, but listed as a 1968 because it used 1968 cosmetics. For some unknown reason, the car missed a planned summer 1968 debut and was not shipped to Washington until October 1968. It was now listed as a "1969" since it was updated with 1969 trim and ornamentation.

The 1968 or 1969 Lincoln Continental parade car showing the unique roof panels. The Secret Service's rear hand-rail and bumper that unfolded into a platform were copied from similar items used on the twin 1968 Lincoln follow-up cars. (Ford Motor Company)

Whether a 1968 or 1969, this "one off" was done by Lehmann-Peterson as an official parade car for the president to supplement the 1961/1964 Lincoln that was still considered the flagship of the White House fleet. Indeed, it still was used by the Nixons for the 1973 inaugural parade.

Lehmann-Peterson had been producing the "stretched" Lincoln Continental Executive Limousine for the Lincoln-Mercury Division since 1964, or 1963 if you count a couple of prototypes. While somewhat similar to the executive limousines in external appearance, there were many differences. For starters, the president's car had a two-inch taller roof and a rear window that was quite a bit larger. There also was a special hinged glass center section and the rear quarter windows that could be hidden by detachable black vinyl covers.

The 1972 Lincoln Continental presidential limousine was patterned after its predecessor, the 1968 presidential limousine, and incorporated many of its features. (Ford Motor Company)

Like the twin 1968 Lincoln Continental four-door convertible follow-up cars, the 1969 presidential Continental used the same fold-down rear bumper design. Hydraulically operated, it provided an 11-inch platform for Secret Service agents who used the handrail for support. The handrail retracted hydraulically into the deck lid when not in use. The 21-foot long, six-ton vehicle built on a 160-inch wheelbase featured a greenhouse-like roof. The center section of the three sections of the president's "moon roof" could be opened and pushed forward so the president and perhaps someone else could stand up and wave to the crowd. The greenhouse was made of a special type of glass paneling developed by PPG Industries--and of course it was bulletproof. A detachable black vinyl cover could be fitted over the entire roof for more formal or private situations. Being a true greenhouse, a special, heavy-duty air conditioning system was required to handle the high heat load from the "greenhouse effect." The system included a dozen outlets, six on either side of the car.

The fender-mounted flags were illuminated by the three tiny spotlights on top of each fender. When the president was riding in the car, the American flag was flown on the right fender and the Presidential Standard was displayed on the left fender. A small Presidential Seal was placed on either side center panel.

The passenger compartment had three rear-facing center seats in addition to the luxurious rear seat. The car was upholstered in a silver-gray pin stripe cloth and vinyl interior similar to that used in the 1968-1/2 Lincoln Continental Mark III. Silver mouton carpeting covered the floor. There were separate front and rear climate control systems and twin two-way communication systems. The car was equipped with a public address system that could be operated in reverse so the occupants could hear the cheers of the crowds outside. The car rode on special 8.90x15 Firestone tires with run-flat capability. Steel discs with rubber edges inside the tires allowed the car to travel at speeds of up to 50 mph even if all four tires were shot out. Reportedly, the armor-plated and bulletproof car cost half a million dollars to build. Reputedly, two tons of armor were built into the car.

The automaker's responsibility does not end when a new car is delivered to the White House. Probably no one gets better "customer service" than the president--usually free or for a nominal fee. As just one example, while visiting Australia, President Johnson's limousine was paint-bombed by protestors and the hood was splattered with paint. Ford had the car repainted and ready for the president within 12 hours.

1972 PRESIDENTIAL CONTINENTAL

The replacement for the famous 1961 "Kennedy Lincoln Continental" was commissioned by the Secret Service in 1970, but would not be delivered to the White House until 1972. The car closely followed the 1969 Lincoln Continental presidential limousine in many of its features. Ford's Special Vehicles Engineering Office was the prime contractor for the car, farming out some of its construction to other companies.

While using the basics of the 1972 Lincoln Town Sedan, the car was stretched to a bumper-to-bumper length of 259 inches with a 161-inch wheelbase and was 61.1 inches tall, meaning a two-and-one-half times taller roof line than production Lincolns. The normal 1972 Lincoln Continental was 225 inches long and had a 127-inch wheelbase. Virtually all of the extra length went into an additional section between the front and rear doors. This section included a combination vinyl panel with an embedded Continental logo and a glass window. A rear "greenhouse" provided better visibility for and of the car's occupants. Naturally, all glass in the car was bulletproof. Unlike regular 1972 four-doors, the presidential car had suicide-type rear doors. The glass-topped roof panels opened so two people could stand during parades. There was a pop-up support to help them keep their balance. The Presidential Seal was located on the rear doors. Two tiny lights on either front fender illuminated the flags displayed when the president was on board.

Interior of the 1972 presidential limousine. The car was done in gray leather and was fitted with both a telephone and microphone for a loudspeaker. (Ford Motor Company)

The rear passenger compartment had three rear-facing folding seats plus the rear seat for the president and his guests. The interior was upholstered in medium-gray leather in essentially the same pattern as in ordinary 1972 Lincoln Continentals with matching nylon carpeting. The exterior was black. The presidential party had fluorescent viewing and reading lamps. There were separate front and rear climate control systems. The chauffeur's section was upholstered in black leather. High-tech communication and security equipment was controlled by a 14-unit aerospace-type master control module. There also was a twin two-way communications system.

The mechanics featured oversized front disc and drum-type rear brakes, dual alternators, a foam bladder fuel tank with reserve pump, added stabilizer bar and 9.54x16.5 Firestone Transport 500 tires. Tie-down points were attached to the frame for use when the car was transported by air. Like earlier Lincoln presidential cars, the rear bumper folded down to provide a platform for Secret Service agents and the pop-up handrail was now hinged near the rear edge of the trunk.

Apparently, President Nixon was quite impressed with the current Lincolns. At his request, a production 1973 Lincoln four-door sedan was given to Leonid I. Brezhnev, then the head man in the Soviet Union and an avid car enthusiast. These huge, luxurious Lincolns epitomized capitalism.

Then Vice-President Richard Nixon riding in a 1958 Edsel convertible during a parade in Lima, Peru. (John Conde)

While Lincolns and Cadillacs get most of the glory during the inauguration of a president, other marques often do yeoman duty in the background. These 1969 AMC Ambassadors with their military drivers served during the inauguration of Richard Nixon. In all, American Motors supplied 53 Ambassador sedans to transport visiting dignitaries. Three all-white Ambassador DPL station wagons were used as emergency vehicles during the parade. (Larry Mitchell Collection)

ANOTHER NIXON LINCOLN

While the Nixon family had many cars through the years, one has achieved some notoriety in recent years. This is Nixon's 1967 Lincoln Continental convertible that was used by the Nixons while they visited their home in San Clemente, California, between 1968 and 1972. The car was purchased in 1992 by the Imperial Palace Auto Collection and was restored by inmates at the Southern Desert Correction Center near Las Vegas. Two dozen inmates, under the supervision of the experts in the Imperial Palace Auto Restoration Shop, put in some 1,400 hours to complete the restoration.

President and Mrs. Ford, Michigan Senator Robert Griffin, and Governor William G. Milliken ride in the National Cherry Festival Parade, Traverse City, Michigan, July 11, 1975. (Gerald Ford Library)

THE FORD'S FORDS

When it came to private vehicles, the Gerald Ford family drove Fords during most of their married life. In later years the Fords bought a Chrysler and a Jeep for one of the Ford children.

Two more presidential Lincoln Continentals were added to the Secret Service's White House fleet in 1974 and another in 1977. The beige 1974 Continental sedan and silver 1977 Continental sedan were pretty ordinary in external appearance. However, according to the Secret Service, they included the security features of the larger contemporary presidential Lincoln limousines. While seldom mentioned, the vice-president also has his own "fleet" of special cars. For example, in the late 1970s, this fleet included a beige 1974 Lincoln sedan and a dark blue 1977 Lincoln sedan.

A young looking Gerald Ford attaching a special license plate promoting Michigan apples to his Ford Customline sedan. (Ford Library)

CHAPTER IX

CARTER THROUGH CLINTON (1977-1995)

TRANSPORTING THE PRESIDENT GETS MORE DIFFICULT

Just as the president's job has become more demanding and difficult, so has the job of transporting him. Besides traveling more frequently to more distant locations around the world, the security of the president has been put in greater jeopardy with each passing administration. By the 1970s, open-top convertibles had virtually disappeared from the White House fleet and by the 1980s, even presidential limousines with opening greenhouse tops or sunroofs had disappeared, as well.

Instead, today the president usually travels pretty much "buttoned-up" in a closed limousine with protective features that rival those of a military armored car--or perhaps even a light tank. While still quite visible, passengers look through large bulletproof windows. Hopefully, the day does not come when the president has to use a real armored car or is completely restricted from public view while traveling.

By the 1980s, America's two producers of luxury cars, Cadillac and Lincoln, were supplying presidential limousines.

This 1979 Cadillac presidential limousine was based on the Fleetwood limousine, but was stretched even more than the versions offered to "civilians." (Jimmy Carter Library)

President Jimmy Carter greets his chauffeur with the Cadillac presidential limousine in the background. (Jimmy Carter Library)

The split duty was partly due to the huge costs involved in building and supporting the special cars, and partly due to fairness, since both companies wanted the prestige and publicity that comes from being seen in the company of the President of the United States. In contrast to the $25,000 needed to buy the entire White House fleet in 1911 or the $8,348.74 spent on the "Sunshine Special" in 1939, the cost of a single presidential limousine had grown to over a half million dollars by the 1970s. Much of the cost comes from the elaborate electronics, communications and protection equipment now installed in the limousines.

1983 CADILLAC PRESIDENTIAL PARADE LIMOUSINE

While still large and impressive, presidential limousines seemed to have lost much of their special character by the 1980s. A prime example is the 1983 Cadillac parade limousine that was delivered to President Reagan in early 1984. Some of the mystique of "stretched" limousines had become lost as limos, often longer and fancier than the president's, had become so common around airports, at weddings and on prom nights. The 1983 presidential parade limousine was based on the Cadillac Fleetwood limousine, then the only mass produced limousine available from any American automaker. The president's version was even longer than the stock Fleetwood limousine. The "stretch" was most obvious from the additional sections and windows added between the front and rear doors. Also, the presidential limousine has a taller top and much larger windows, including a large rear window. Unlike the typical private limousine buyer who wants the privacy, the president usually wants to be seen.

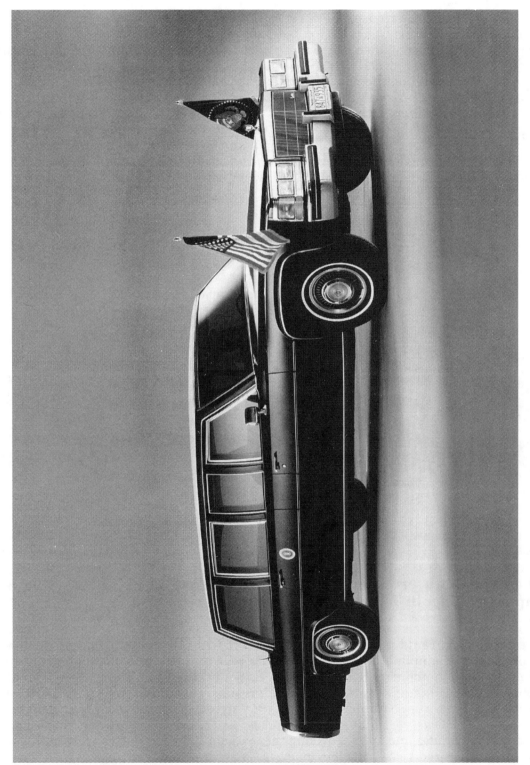

1983 Cadillac parade limousine delivered during the Reagan administration. (O'AGara-Hess & Eisenhardt)

1989 LINCOLN PRESIDENTIAL PARADE LIMOUSINE

When George Bush was inaugurated in January 1989, he rode in a brand new Lincoln presidential parade limousine. While delivered a few months earlier to President Reagan and President-elect Bush at the White House, the car was not officially used until Inauguration Day. The car had been conceived five years before and took just under three years to build. The 22-foot long, custom-built Lincoln Town Car was designed and built at Ford's Advanced Vehicle Development facility in Dearborn Heights, Michigan. The one-of-a-kind parade car retained the interior and exterior styling theme of the production Lincoln Town Car. While starting out production as a 1989 Lincoln Town Car, it was disassembled, then completely rebuilt from the ground up. The wheelbase was increased by 44.7 inches (from 117.3 to 162 inches) and the overall length was now 263.7 inches. Like other Cadillac Lincoln parade cars, the roof was raised, in this case two-and-one-half inches higher than the regular production Lincoln Town Car. As in the past, armoring was again provided by O'Gara-Hess & Eisenhardt. Special hooks were welded onto the chassis to tie down the car when it was transported by air around the world.

The 1989 custom-built presidential limousine was built by Ford starting with a contemporary Lincoln Town Car. (Ford Motor Company)

The rear compartment could hold six people in comfort with three on the folding jump seats facing the president. The midnight black car had its rear compartment done in shadow blue cloth and leather with matching plush blue nylon carpet on the floor. The leather trim above the top of the jump seats featured an embroidered "presidential edition" logo. Two more "presidential edition" emblems were embedded in the black vinyl covering the roof pillar between the two compartments. A powered, sliding glass window separated the front and rear compartments. For daytime parades and special events, the president and his guests were quite visible inside due to the oversized rear-quarter windows. At night, fluorescent lights with specially molded lens covers illuminated the interior. Separate heating and air conditioning units for the front and rear compartments automatically monitored and maintained the comfort level for passengers.

The interior of the 1989 Lincoln presidential limousine, which is trimmed with shadow-blue cloth and matching plush nylon carpet. (Ford Motor Company)

The modifications significantly increased the vehicle's weight, requiring a completely redesigned chassis. There was also a 7.5 liter (460 cid) V-8 from Ford's truck line that was fitted with a dual exhaust system using specially built stainless-steel mufflers and exhaust pipes. A C-6 automatic transmission and a heavy-duty rear axle were used, as well as larger wheels and brakes. To prevent any possible danger due to a bullet or shrapnel rupturing the stainless steel fuel tank and causing a fire, the tank was filled with a special foam, a technique used on military aircraft and race cars.

The "White House on Wheels" incorporated much advanced security and communications equipment. For instance, there was a multifunction message center control module in the driver compartment, twin two-way communications system and a public address system.

1993 CADILLAC FLEETWOOD BROUGHAM - PRESIDENTIAL EDITION

The latest presidential limousine was delivered to the White House in early 1993, just about the time the Clinton family was moving in. Actually, three identical presidential limousines were built by Cadillac for the president and his family. Officially, the trio are designated "Cadillac Fleetwood Brougham-Presidential Series." Unlike most previous specials for the first family that combined the efforts of both an automaker and outside contractors, all facets of the design, development and manufacture were completed totally within General Motors. Of course, the entire project was conducted under the close supervision of the Secret Service.

The latest 1993 Cadillac presidential limousine provides more protection. As a consequence the president is far less visible than in parade cars of the past, especially the open top ones used before the JFK assassination. (Cadillac)

Based on Cadillac's redesigned Fleetwood series, the limousines' special chassis and powertrain were designed and built by the Cadillac Motor Car Division and GM's Powertrain Division with help from General Motors' Advanced Engineering Staff. Modifications included stretching the chassis to a total length of 270 inches on a 167.5-inch long wheelbase. This compares to the Fleetwood Brougham's normal length of 225.1 inches and 121.5-inch wheelbase.

The 1993 Cadillac presidential limousines are nine inches longer than the previous Cadillac presidential limousine delivered to Ronald Reagan in 1984. GM's Cadillac Design Studio developed the body's exterior and interior design. The exterior styling combines standard Fleetwood Brougham sheet metal and trim with special body and trim features. For instance, the roof was raised three inches compared to production Fleetwood Broughams in order to provide a distinctly large glass area so the president is visible to the maximum extent possible during parades and ceremonial occasions. A special 12-volt fluorescent halo-lighting system aids nighttime visibility of the interior.

Similar to other recent presidential limousines, there are no provisions like an opening roof whereby the president can stand and wave to the crowds. Today, the Secret Service believes such exposure is much too dangerous. Likewise, Secret Service agents must walk alongside, or ride in the follow-up vehicles, since unlike presidential limousines of the past, there are no hidden runningboards. The car is painted in black clearcoat with small Presidential Seal decals on the rear doors. Twin flush-mounted spotlights located in the fenders illuminate the flags at night.

Like other recent presidential limousines, there is seating for six people in the rear compartment when the three flush-folding seats are used. Both compartments of the car are upholstered in a combination of dark blue cloth and leather with tasteful Zebrano wood accents. Embroidered Presidential Seals are affixed to each rear passenger door, as well as to the center of the rear seat.

A special partition separates the driver and passenger compartments. A power window in the partition can be lowered by the front seat occupants. There are separate and individually controlled heating and air conditioning units for the front and rear compartments. There are also separate front and rear Delco AM/FM/stereo cassette enter-systems with a dozen premium two-way speakers; eight speakers are in the rear compartment with four up front. In the rear, both the climate control and entertainment systems are housed in an overhead console. The special communications system includes a public address system and telephone.

The limousines' body structures and special armoring systems were designed by Cadillac Engineering and built by GM's Parts Fabrication. Like other Fleetwood Broughams, the presidential versions use a 5.7 liter (350 cid) V-8 engine and a four-speed automatic transmission. The driver can keep tabs on engine operation via custom engine monitoring gauges mounted in the instrument panel next to the standard Cadillac instrument cluster. Because of the substantially increased weight, the limousines are equipped with a beefed-up power brake system and oversized wheels and tires.

BILL CLINTON'S MUSTANG

Like many of the "Sixties Generation" President Bill Clinton owns a Mustang--one of the most popular cars of the 1960s. Clinton acquired the 1967 ice-blue Mustang convertible while he was still governor of Arkansas. Actually, the Mustang was in the Clinton family for many years. In 1972, President Clinton's late stepfather, Jeff Dwire, bought the car for Bill's younger brother, Roger Clinton, when the Clinton family lived in Hot Springs, Arkansas. At the time, Roger was 16 years old and Bill was in law school at Yale. When Bill and Hillary Clinton acquired the car, they had the car's exterior and interior refurbished. While living in the Arkansas Governor's Mansion, he liked to take the Mustang out for Sunday afternoon drives with his family.

The Mustang was also used in the 1992 presidential campaign. On August 19, 1992, Arkansas friends hosted a birthday party with a '50s and '60s theme. Hillary Rodham Clinton and Chelsea Clinton arrived with Bill in the 1967 Mustang. Bill, dressed in '60s garb of blue jeans, black sweater, and a favorite pair of sunglasses, drove the family to the event.

President Clinton enjoys a brief ride in his blue 1967 Mustang convertible. (Cranford Johnson Robinson Wood)

During the 1920s and early 1930s, Pierce-Arrow was arguably America's most prestigious marque. Thus it was no surprise that the White House fleet had several. This handsome 1917 Pierce-Arrow Model A4-66 was used by President Wilson between 1917 and 1918. (Imperial Palace Hotel & Casino)

This bulletproof and armor-plated 1936 V-16 Cadillac was used by President Roosevelt. It is shown as it was purchased by the Imperial Palace and Casino's Antique & Classic Car Collection several years ago. It was completely restored and is now part of the Presidential Row Display. (Imperial Palace Hotel & Casino)

This specially-built 1940 Willys-Overland convertible was a gift from Eleanor Roosevelt's brother, G. Hall Roosevelt. Like several other cars, it was fitted with hand controls so FDR could drive it at the Little White House. (Georgia Department of Natural Resources, Division of State Parks & Historic Sites)

The 1941 Chrysler Royal coupe purchased by Senator Harry S. Truman and driven by him until he became president in 1945. (Courtesy Harry S. Truman Library)

The 1941 Chrysler Windsor four-door sedan used by Mrs. Harry Truman. (Charles Jensen)

Famed coachbuilder J.J. Derham reworked the rear windows on the 1955 Crown Imperial limousine so that they provided a more open, hardtop-like appearance to the rear compartment. The 1955 Imperial is still owned by Jim Jones who bought it after its White House duties were finished. (Alice M. Starke)

This 1974 Lincoln presidential limousine converted by Hess & Eisenhardt served the Nixon, Ford, Carter, and Reagan administrations. (O'Gara-Hess & Eisenhardt)

President and Mrs. Reagan greeting the crowd through the roof of the 1972 Lincoln Parade Car. (White House)

The 1993 presidential limousine based on the Cadillac Fleetwood Brougham. (Cadillac)

Lincolns have been by far the most popular starting point for special limousines for the president. This 1989 presidential limousine built by Ford and Hess & Eisenhardt represents the latest in the string of special Lincolns that date back to the FDR administration. (O'Gara - Hess & Eisenhardt)

President Bill Clinton with "Marine Corps One" in the background. (White House)

The VC-137C, "Air Force One" in flight. (White House)

"Marine One" is a Sikorsky VH-37D, the military version of the Sikorsky S-61. (Joyce C Naltchavan, White House)

When the president travels long distances today it is aboard one of two Boeing 747s. The aircraft is officially called "Air Force One" only when the president is aboard. (U.S.A.F.)

This huge "hangar" at Andrews Air Force Base can handle both of the new "Air Force One" jumbo jets plus a couple smaller aircraft. (Daniel Mann, Johnson and Mendenhall)

Famous American Personalities and Memorable Fords, Lincolns, and Mercurys
(Courtesy of Ford Motor Company)

1950 Presidential Lincoln Cosmopolitan

Car of the state — The Ford-built Lincoln automobile has been a long-standing favorite of American presidents. Roosevelt had his famous 1939 "Sunshine Special" and when it was retired this specially-built limousine on a 1950 Lincoln Cosmopolitan chassis replaced it. The car served presidents Truman, Eisenhower, and Kennedy and was fondly called the "Bubble-top" for its familiar plexiglass parade canopy installed during Eisenhower's term. Its last state appearance was a summit meeting between Kruschev and Kennedy in Vienna.

1936 Ford Phaeton

Ford fan — President Franklin D. Roosevelt and Henry Ford were always at odds over government controls imposed by the National Recovery Act (NRA) of 1933 but the chief executive remained a loyal Ford car owner. Though crippled with polio, he enjoyed driving at his Hyde Park, New York, estate and at his country home in Warm Springs, Georgia, where he kept a 1938 Ford Convertible Sedan (show inset). At both places he had Ford V8's fitted with hand controls and he is pictured in 1937 touring Hyde Park with one of his favorites.

1946 Ford Super Deluxe Tudor Sedan

Harry's new Ford — Americans had gone without new cars for the duration of World War II and as the end drew near, Ford Motor Company was the first auto maker to resume civilian production. A beaming President Harry S. Truman proudly accepted the first car produced from young Henry Ford II at the White House. The austere spotlight-equipped V8 sedan was built July 3, 1945 — two months before the end of all hostilities.

Some Of The Presidential Vehicles In "Presidential Row Display" At The Imperial Palace Antique And Classic Collection In Las Vegas, Nevada.

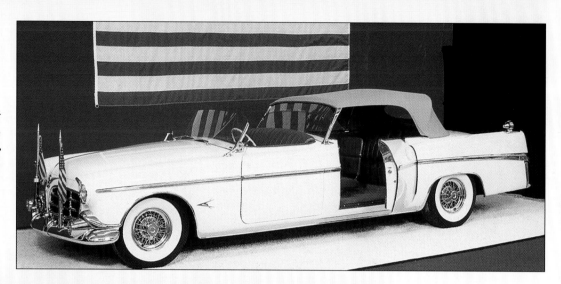

Dwight Eisenhower's 1952 Chrysler Imperial.

John F. Kennedy's 1962 Lincoln Continental.

Lyndon Johnson's 1964 Cadillac Limousine.

CHAPTER X

THE PRESIDENT TAKES TO THE AIR

FROM FLYING BOATS TO JUMBO JETS

"Air Force One," with its Presidential Seal near the door and big American flags on the tail, has become a familiar sight to people around the world. In the last half century, air transportation for the president has come a long way from the day when a presidential flight made history. Today a presidential flight is as common as a ride in his limousine. Flying has become a way of life for the president who can, and has, circled the globe for a conference with other heads of state.

FDR WAS THE FIRST PRESIDENT TO FLY

American presidents have been flying for almost half a century with Franklin Delano Roosevelt being the first president to fly while in office. Technically, Teddy Roosevelt holds the distinction of being the first president to fly, but his ride was in October 1910, long after he had left office. The event took place at the Aero Club in St. Louis' Aviation Field. Teddy Roosevelt took to the air in the Wright Brothers Type B pusher airplane for a flight that lasted a mere four minutes and reached an altitude of only 50 feet.

The first "official" presidential air trip occurred in the midst of World War II when FDR took off on January 11, 1943, from a seaplane base near Miami for Casablanca, Morocco. The historic flight would precede an equally historic event: FDR's meeting with Prime Minister Winston Churchill and French General Charles de Gaulle, to plan the invasion of southern Europe.

The first presidential takeoff was made aboard one of the famous Pan American Clippers. The Navy had contracted for the use of several of these Clippers during the war. The "Dixie Clipper" flew the over-water legs of the journey. The "Atlantic Clipper," an identical Pan American Clipper, flew along as an escort and served as a communications center so that President Roosevelt could keep track of happenings in Washington, as well as on the war front in both Europe and the Pacific. The over-land portions of the trip were made with four-engined C-54s flown by TWA crews.

The "Dixie Clipper" carried few of the luxury items that might be expected aboard a presidential aircraft. About the only special request was that one berth be equipped with a double mattress. Also, extra supplies of linen and a few upholstered chairs were put aboard. The plane wore the appropriate wartime camouflage paint job.

Navy Lt. Howard M. Cone and his 10-man crew were told they would be carrying an important person aboard the "Dixie Clipper," but they never imagined it would be the President of the United States. Lieutenant Cone was told only that he would be carrying nine passengers who were listed as number one, number two, etc. When passenger number one stepped into the Clipper's lounge, Lieutenant Cone nervously snapped a salute and somehow found the right words: 'Mr. President. I'm glad to have you aboard, sir.'

General Eisenhower chats with FDR aboard a C-54. (Roosevelt Library)

Besides being the first flight by a president while in office, the trip made some other history. No other president had traveled to Africa or had left the United States during wartime. And no president since Abraham Lincoln had visited a battlefield during war. The trip had another highlight that would be remembered by the crew; President Roosevelt celebrated his 61st birthday aboard the Clipper. Everyone, with the exception of pilot Lieutenant Cone, toasted FDR with champagne. Someone had even smuggled aboard a birthday cake.

The first presidential flight was considered a tremendous success. In the trip to and from Casablanca, the two Clippers covered 11,000 miles without incident. They were in the air almost three full days, touched down on three continents, crossed the Equator four times and the Atlantic twice. Today, a similar trip aboard "Air Force One" would take about seven hours. Not until the two Clippers reached their moorings in New York and dropped off their passengers in Miami, were all the personnel involved in the operation told that they had helped fly the president.

As previously mentioned, FDR transferred from the flying boat to a C-54 for the over-land portions of the journey. After the 10-day conference at Casablanca, FDR made a 2,000 mile side trip to Liberia, using two C-54s piloted by TWA crews. Army Air Corps Major Otis F. Bryan, a TWA vice-president in civilian life, had the honor of being the presidential pilot for this trip.

"GUESS WHERE II"

As any war buff will tell you, the B-24 Liberator was one of the real fighting ladies of World War II. Along with the B-17 Flying Fortress, the B-24s participated in many of the important bombing raids over occupied Europe. Therefore, a transport based on this bomber would seem to be an unlikely candidate for a presidential aircraft. However, the officials thought otherwise. Thus in 1943, a plane that from the outside looked like a B-24, appeared at Washington's National Airport to take up the job of flying the president.

This airplane had started out as a C-87 Liberator Express, the cargo transport version of the B-24. Unlike the B-24, the C-87 carried its fuel in the wings. The interior of the plane had been modified from stem to stern to accommodate the chief executive, yet from the outside it still looked like a standard wartime bomber--but without guns. Even though the "Guess Where II," a name given to it by its pilot, was never to actually fly the president, its accommodations set the precedent for the luxury to be found in future presidential aircraft.

The fat fuselage of the Liberator looked a lot like today's jumbo jets. Nothing was spared in making the cavernous interior as convenient as possible. Along the right side of the plane were four compartments that could be converted for sleeping. There was a complete kitchen and two lavatories, and even a large davenport for in-flight conferences.

One of the reasons why this airplane never got to fly the president was the tail vibration problems the B-24s were experiencing at the time the aircraft was delivered. A B-24 had crashed due to this vibration problem, causing great concern about its ability to fly the president safely. Although the problem turned out to be minor and easily fixed, the C-54 never got to transport the president.

However, during its lifetime, the converted bomber transported many other VIPs, including the First Lady, Eleanor Roosevelt. In 1944, "Guess Where II" was returned to more mundane duties, never having done the job for which it was built. No trumpets sounded in October 1945, when the "Guess Where II" made its final flight and eventually was cut up for scrap. It was indeed sad that this one-of-a-kind airplane was not saved so that future generations could see the first plane modified to carry the president.

"THE SACRED COW"

FDR's trip to Casablanca had proved that presidential air travel was not only possible, but desirable. Therefore it became apparent that the president needed his own special aircraft. Project 51, as the classified project was called, directed the Douglas Aircraft Company to build a new airplane for the president. Since extreme care and security was used in its construction, the plane was put together in a secluded part of the Douglas plant and the workmen were watched closely by both civilian and military inspectors.

President Roosevelt's crippled condition was a paramount consideration in designing the interior. Some rather elaborate modifications, including a set of removable steel rails, were added so FDR could move about the C-54 in a special wheelchair. The modifications allowed access to the cockpit where FDR could sit between the pilot and co-pilot.

The interior decor was not quite as luxurious as today's private executive aircraft, but it was not far behind. Some of the more interesting furnishings included a spacious presidential stateroom with a conference table, interplane telephone, upholstered swivel chair, fold-out sofa bed and two electrically operated folding chairs. An instrument panel in the cabin included an airspeed indicator, compass, clock and altimeter. President Roosevelt wanted them to track the aircraft's progress. There were three other staterooms for FDR's traveling companions.

It was realized that special wheelchair ramps around an airport would be a dead giveaway that FDR would be using that particular airfield. During wartime, this would become a risky situation. So a special battery-operated elevator was installed, which brought its passenger from the ground to cabin-floor height in one easy motion. This neat system did away with the need for telltale ramps. A large bulletproof picture window was installed near the front of the plane so that the president could see outside. Interestingly enough, this was the only "armor-plated" portion of the craft. The rest of the plane was made of normal, thin aluminum and was hardly a match for even a small caliber bullet.

"Looking like any other C-54" was one of the most important thoughts in the designers' minds. The elevator modification did not show, and a special template was constructed to place over the bulletproof window to make it look like a regular C-54 window. There were no fancy trappings on the outside of the plane, just the normal military markings. It certainly was a far cry from the snappily painted presidential planes that were to follow in the future.

The airplane was dubbed the "Sacred Cow" by Washington news correspondents. Official circles tried to discourage the use of this nickname, but with no luck. The "Sacred Cow" nickname never was painted on the bird nor was it ever accepted officially. After all the work that had gone into the "Sacred Cow," FDR would use it only once before his death in 1945. This occasion was during his trek from Malta to Yalta, a trip during which the famous passenger traveled under the codename "Sawbuck" for security reasons.

The C-54 was unofficially called the "Sacred Cow." It flew President Roosevelt only once, but the 44 flags on the fuselage denoted the other nations to which it flew diplomatic and VIP flights during World War II. (US Navy/Truman Library)

The "Independence" had a distinctive paint job. (US Navy/Truman Library)

Actually, President Roosevelt took only three air trips while in office. Even in the mid-1940s, air travel was a novelty for most Americans, even the president of the United States--a sharp contrast with latter presidents for whom flying has become an almost an everyday occurrence.

After FDR's death, the "Sacred Cow" remained unchanged for its new master, Harry Truman. Even the now unneeded elevator was retained. Somehow, it just did not seem right to remove it. When the war ended, it was decided to decorate the "Sacred Cow" for its many trips carrying dignitaries around the world. Forty-four flags were painted on the nose to signify the countries the plane had touched down in during its important missions. Just like the fighters and bombers that heralded their "kills," the "Sacred Cow" showed the world how it had served the United States.

In 1947 the "Sacred Cow" bid farewell to its White House duties and for the first time joined its C-54 brothers in the "real" Air Force. During its presidential tour, it had flown 1900 hours and more than 425,000 air miles.

HARRY TRUMAN'S "INDEPENDENCE"

The next presidential airplane, also built by Douglas, was a DC-6 similar to those used by the airlines in the 1950s and 1960s. At the time, the four-engine aircraft was the most modern, long-range propeller air transport with the then-amazing speed of 350 mph. The plane quickly was dubbed the "Independence" before she got a more undignified name such as the "Sacred Cow." The presidential pilot, Army Air Forces Lt. Col. Henry Myers, chose this name for two good reasons. The plane was put into service on Independence Day, 1947, and Mr. Truman's hometown was Independence, Missouri.

Harry Truman disembarking from the "Independence." (USAF/Truman Library)

Officially, the "Independence," a military version of the DC-6, was designated by the Air Force as a C-118 with tail number 6505. The "Independence" had all the latest aircraft innovations of the day, including reversible pitch propellers, water injection for extra power during takeoff and weather avoidance radar.

It also had the jazziest paint job of any presidential transport. The theme of the paint job was the American Eagle, the national bird. The yellow nose suggested a beak and the cockpit looked like the eagle's head with the windows simulating eyes. Narrow lines on the front fuselage hinted of a mouth and there were three blue feathers outlined in yellow on the tail. The fuselage was painted in two-tone blue. The paint scheme originally had been intended for American Airlines, but the company gave it to the planners of the "Independence," who fell in love with it. Unfortunately, the Air Force could not come up with the $1,500 to pay Douglas for the extra frill. But Douglas finally threw in the paint job for free.

The "Independence" served with honor for five-and-one-half years before removing her presidential markings and going back to being a regular Air Force C-118 transport. However, even with the Air Force she was something special. In 1953 she received four new engines. With the new engines she would set an unofficial speed record on a trip from California to Washington, D.C., thus becoming the fastest transport in her day.

The "Columbine" was a Lockheed Constellation used by Dwight Eisenhower while in office. (Eisenhower Library)

IKE'S "COLUMBINE"

The replacement for the "Independence" was probably the sleekest and most graceful propeller-driven airplane ever built--the four-engine Lockheed Constellation. With the inauguration of Dwight D. Eisenhower as president in 1953, a "Connie" became the official residential aircraft. Tail number 448-610 carried the interesting name of "Columbine II." During his military days, General Eisenhower had become partial to Connies. In fact, the first "Columbine," a "Connie," had served him well when he was commanding SHAPE. So it was not surprising that he selected the Constellation for presidential duties.

President Eisenhower leaving the Aero Commander used to shuttle him to his Gettysburg farm. (Eisenhower Library)

The name "Columbine" was reportedly chosen by Mamie Eisenhower because the columbine was the state flower of Colorado, the first lady's home state. By 1954 the rapid progress in aircraft technology had caught up with the "Columbine II." She was replaced by a later model Lockheed Constellation that had greater speed, could carry more and could travel further before having to refuel. This new "Connie," tail number 53-7885, carried on the tradition and was dubbed the "Columbine III." She carried important improvements needed to keep in touch with the president at all times, including an airborne teletype machine and an air-to-ground telephone with which Ike could keep in constant communication with the White House.

The "Columbine III" served the president for six years, then the longest of any presidential aircraft. While the "Columbine" was used on all of Ike's domestic trips, by the end of his second term, Ike was using USAF jet-powered transports on his four overseas trips. These included one trip during which he visited England, France and West Germany. A second trip was made to 11 nations in Europe, Asia, the Middle East and Africa. A third trip was made to South America and on yet another he went to the Far East.

When Ike, a pilot himself, purchased a farm in Gettysburg, he quickly tired of the two-hour drive from Washington. Therefore, he saw that a light plane could cut the trip to a half-hour. Up until 1955, the Secret Service had insisted that the president needed the safety of four engines and the grass strip near Gettysburg could not support the "Columbine." Thus, it took some persuasion to get an Aero Commander like those already in service with the Army. When flying in the Aero Commander, Ike was accompanied by his Secret Service protectors flying in a similar plane. After the first year, this presidential Aero Commander was replaced with a later model with better performance. This new plane served Ike until he left office in 1961. The Aero Commanders never received "official" status of presidential aircraft, however.

John Kennedy getting briefed en route aboard "Air Force One." (Kennedy Library)

One of the most historic photos ever--Lyndon Johnson being sworn in aboard "Air Force One" after President Kennedy was assassinated. (Johnson Library)

"AIR FORCE ONE"

Presidential air travel entered the "jet age" when the Boeing 707 became the presidential aircraft in 1962. Actually, jetliners had already become commonplace by the time the president could routinely suffer from "jet lag." The prototype for the 707, the Boeing 367-80, made its maiden flight in July 1954. The first 707 went into service with Pan Am in October 1958.

In official parlance, "Air Force One" is a VC-137, the V for "very important person" and the C for "cargo," a fitting description for the president. Actually, now any aircraft carrying the president is called "Air Force One," an identifier used by pilots and air traffic controllers in their radio communications. The second "Air Force One" was added to the presidential air fleet in 1972. They have served eight presidents including: Kennedy, Johnson, Nixon, Ford, Carter, Reagan, Bush and Clinton.

"Air Force One" even has the dubious honor of being the first aircraft to "host" an inauguration when Lyndon Baines Johnson was hastily sworn in after JFK was assassinated in Dallas. LBJ's first "executive order" after being sworn in by Federal Judge Sarah T. Hughes was "Now,

LBJ in conference aboard "Air Force One." (Johnson Library)

let's get airborne."

While Jackie Kennedy was the first lady, she not only directed the redecoration of the White House, she also was the person who selected the attractive color scheme found on the presidential jets. The interior facilities and equipment found within tail number 26000 are unbelievable. Nothing is spared in making the president's flight comfortable and pleasant. However, when the president flies, he has little time for gazing out the window. In flight, the president usually is conducting important business, just as he would if he were at his desk in the White House. To help make working and talking easy, 26000 was built to be the quietest aircraft in the sky.

During the Nixon administration, the presidential aircraft were also nicknamed "Spirit of '76." President Nixon flew on 26000 on his historic trip to the People's Republic of China in February 1972, as well as to the U.S.S.R. a few months later. On one trip aboard the replacement 27000 former Presidents Nixon, Ford and Carter flew to Cairo, Egypt, in 1981 to represent the United States at the funeral of Egyptian President Anwar Sadat.

"MARINE CORPS ONE"

Perhaps as familiar to most Americans is "Marine One," the helicopter that takes off from the lawn of the White House for short hops and for the first leg of longer journeys. President Eisenhower made the first historic helicopter flight in September 1957, when he was called back to Washington on short notice. The short trip aboard a Marine Helicopter Squadron One (HMX-1) UH-34 helicopter took him from Newport, Rhode Island, where he was vacationing to the Quonset Point Naval Station where he continued to the Capitol aboard a fixed-wing aircraft. The flight showed the usefulness of helicopters and President Eisenhower continued to use them during the rest of his administration.

"Marine One" is currently a Sikorsky-built VH-3D that has been modified for the president's special needs. This includes sophisticated onboard communications equipment that allows the president and his staff continuous access to all essential government agencies. The VH-3D cruises at 110 knots (131 mph) and has a range of around 500 miles.

Marine Helicopter Squadron One also flies the president on a VH-60N, the "executive" version of the Sikorsky-built UH-60 "Blackhawk" troop-carrying helicopter. The VH-60N is fitted with a comfortable interior and special communications package that is quite comparable to that on the VH-3D. Because the VH-60 is smaller and easier to transport, it is ideal for use overseas. While the president flies on "Marine One" the White House staff and the press entourage can travel on three other VIP helicopters operated by the Marines of HMX-1. These currently include a CH-46E, CH-53D, and CH-53E.

"Marine One," the president's helicopter, not only operates around Washington, but virtually anywhere the president travels, including overseas trips. To date it has been used in 32 countries and landed at such exotic locations as Windsor Castle in England, Akasaka Palace in Tokyo, Bolivar Square in Bogota, Columbia, and even in the Demilitarized Zone in South Korea. HMX1 not only provides helicopter service for the president, but also the vice-president, members of the Cabinet and foreign dignitaries.

NEW "AIR FORCE ONES"

After over a quarter century of duty, the Boeing 707-based "Air Force One" had become quite obsolete by the 1990s. Indeed, by then most Boeing 707s had already been phased out of first-line commercial service. Thus the spare parts supply was drying up and these aging aircraft required greatly increased maintenance to keep them flying. Near the end, the old "Air Force Ones" did not even meet all the then-current FAA standards.

The latest "Air Force Ones" are based on the wide-body Boeing 747-200B jumbo jet. The new "Air Force Ones," given the military designation VC-25A, are 231 feet long and six stories tall. Inside, there are some 4,000 square feet of interior room, almost twice that of the average home. While basically commercial 747s, the aircraft are extensively modified to meet the

The latest "Air Force One" is based on the Boeing 747 "Jumbo Jet." (United States Air Force)

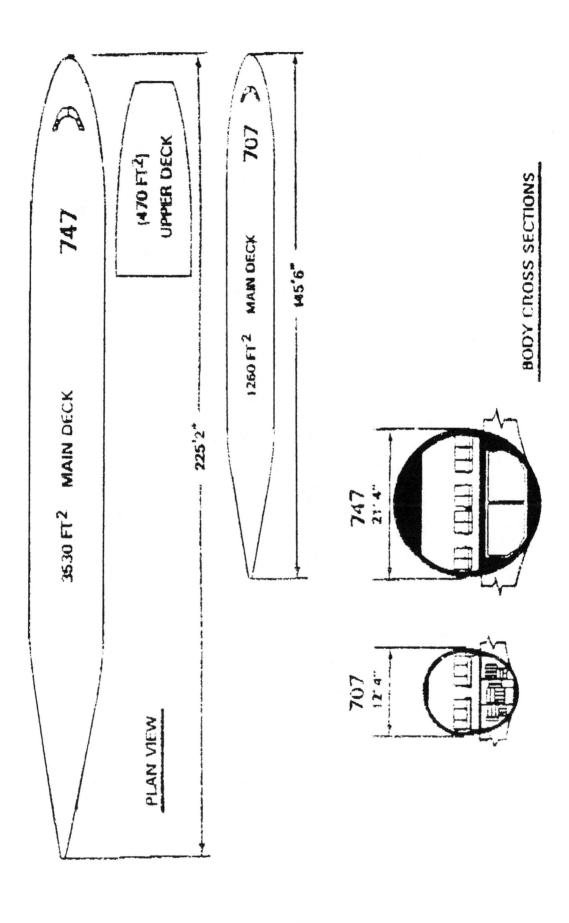

747

PLAN VIEW

3530 FT² MAIN DECK

(470 FT²) UPPER DECK

225'2"

707

1250 FT² MAIN DECK

145'6"

BODY CROSS SECTIONS

747 21'4"

707 12'4"

Comparison between the Boeing 707 and Boeing 747. The bottom line: The president and all his traveling "companions" have significantly more room aboard the latest "Air Force Ones."

Some of the modifications include the presidential suite with an office and stateroom. The stateroom includes a dressing room and lavatory with a shower. The president's flying office includes a large conference room with a VCR, projection screens and a large conference table. The aircraft is loaded with all types of office equipment, from computers and fax machines to copiers and TVs. The aircraft have the latest technology communications and electronics gear so that the president can carry out all his responsibilities while airborne. The onboard communications gear includes state-of-the-art secure voice terminals and cryptographic equipment for writing and deciphering classified messages. All the electronics and communications gear results in some 238 miles of wiring, more than twice the amount found in a typical commercial 747.

Other separate accommodations are provided for guests, senior staff, Secret Service and security personnel, and of course, the news media. The president's quarters are the plushest and most extensive. Couches in the sitting room can be converted into a bed, floors are covered with deep-pile carpet and even the window shades are electrically powered. The aircraft's two galleys are each capable of feeding all the people traveling aboard "Air Force One," and a few more. Indeed, they can provide up to 100 meals at one sitting. There are six passenger lavatories--including handicap facilities. The air crew has their own rest area and mini-galley.

The new "Air Force One" is able to carry up to 73 passengers, plus a 22-person crew. This compares to 46 passengers and a 17-member crew on the previous 707s. The VC-25A can cruise at speeds of up to 630 mph (.92 Mach) at altitudes of up to 45,100 feet. The 747, with its much greater fuel capacity, can fly 9,600 statute miles without refueling, since stops in foreign countries can be a real security headache. Further self-sufficiency is obtained through self-contained fore and aft air stairs and a second auxiliary power unit in the aircraft's tail. The lower portion has been modified to include the self-contained stairs, storage compartments for substantial amounts of food and mission-related equipment and even a self-contained baggage loader.

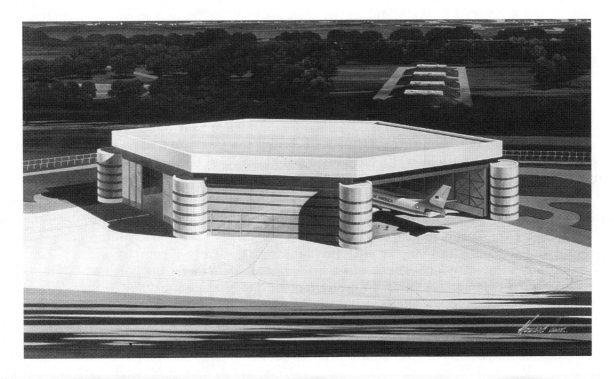

The "Air Force One Maintenance Support Complex" at Andrews AFB, Maryland. (Daniel Mann, Johnson, and Mendenhall)

Built before the end of the Cold War, the aircraft were "hardened" to protect the communication gear from being disrupted by an electromagnetic pulse (EMP), caused by the detonation of nuclear weapons. The emergency medical treatment facility includes a fold-out operating table. Planning for every conceivable eventuality, there are two intravenous hookups in the ceiling of the president's bedroom, should the nation's chief executive become ill in-flight. Perhaps remembering the JFK assassination, the new "Air Force One" even had tie-downs for a casket and one of the aircraft's doors was sized so a coffin could be maneuvered inside.

While built by Boeing Commercial Airplanes in Everett, Washington, the aircraft were flown to Boeing Military Airplane facilities in Wichita, Kansas, for the modifications needed to make them "Air Force Ones." The two 747s cost nearly $650 million. Along with the new aircraft, there is a new "Air Force One Maintenance Support Complex" located at Andrews Air Force Base, about five miles from Washington. The huge "hanger" can handle both 747s, plus an additional aircraft or two. Besides maintenance functions, the complex has a flight kitchen that can prepare as many as 4,000 meals for extended trips. The facility cost only an extra $50 million.

Original plans were to have the two new aircraft in service in 1989, but the program was delayed because of budgetary limitations. The first VC-25A, tail number 28000, flew as "Air Force One" for the first time in September 1990. It was transporting President George Bush on a trip to Kansas, then Florida, and back to Washington, D.C.

The most important component in flying the president is the group of men responsible for maintaining and flying the presidential aircraft. Needless to say, the military people serving in this duty are hand-picked, and they are the best. For instance, the aircraft commanders are highly skilled pilots with a minimum of 4,000 hours of flying all types of airplanes. The presidential pilot is in charge of all aspects of the flight--the airplane, flight plans, ground operations and security. He is supported by all the members of the 89th Military Airlift Wing stationed at Andrews AFB, Maryland, for whom a presidential flight is a routine occurrence.

"DOOMSDAY" AIRPLANE

This specially equipped Boeing 747 wide-body jetliner was thankfully never needed. The purpose of the Doomsday aircraft--there were actually three copies--was as a command post for the nation's commander-in-chief should a large-scale nuclear war have broken out. If conditions had escalated beyond a certain threshold during the Cold War, when the United States and the U.S.S.R. had nuclear warheads aimed at one another, the president would have been whisked to Andrews AFB to board one of the Doomsday aircraft.

After taking off, the aircraft would fly above to maintain command of U.S. military forces, even if a holocaust had occurred on the ground. The largest portion of these aircrafts' interiors is taken up by the battle-staff area. This area is where military and civilian experts study, interpret and condense incoming intelligence data from a variety of sources before passing on the situation to the president. There was a briefing room outside of the battle-staff area with seating for 21 people and the latest in projection equipment. The president's office was in the front of the aircraft directly under the cockpit. This compartment was fitted with a sofa, desk, two bunkbeds and two phones; a white one was for normal communications and a red one scrambled the conversation so it could not be understood if intercepted by the other side. There was a small conference room with a table and nine chairs, one of course, for the president. The aircraft was loaded with sophisticated electronics gear. There were also other seats, bunks and a galley for the aircraft's occupants.

APPENDIX A

FOR FURTHER READING

Cadillac Standard of the World: The Complete History, by Maurice D. Hendry, Automobile Quarterly Publications, 1979. Some information on presidential Cadillacs.

The Cars of Lincoln-Mercury, by George H. Dammann and James K. Wagner, Crestline Publishing, 1987. Good description of Lincolns specially built for the White House fleet from the 1937 "Sunshine Special" to the 1972 Lincoln Continental Parade car. One or more photos of each.

Cars With Personalities, by John A. Conde, Keego Harbor, MI, 1982. Hundreds of photos of cars of the 1896 through early 1970 period shown with famous people including U.S. presidents. Besides captions identifying photos, there are brief introductions to chapters and commentaries.

Illustrated Lincoln Buyer's Guide, by R. Woudenberg, Motorbooks International, 1990. Includes photographs and descriptions of specially built Lincolns from the "Sunshine Special" to the 1972 presidential limousine.

The Lincoln Motorcar: Sixty Years of Excellence, by Thomas E. Bonsall, Baltimore, MD Bookman Publishing, 1981. Ten-page chapter, "America's Motorcar of State" covers Lincolns used by the U.S. president as well as other heads of state.

Presidents on Wheels, by Herbert Ridgeway Collins, New York Bonanza Books, 1971. President-by-president description of how presidents from Washington to Nixon traveled. Covers their horses, carriages and then their cars.

The Truman Cars, by Paul Hartman, Independence, MO Independence Press, 1989. Excellent coverage in words and photographs of the cars used by Harry and Bess Truman in public and private life.

World Book of America's Presidents; Volume II - The President's World, Chicago, IL World Book, Inc. Good chapters covering "Guarding the President's Life" and "On the Road with the President."

APPENDIX B

WHERE YOU CAN SEE PRESIDENTIAL TRANSPORT

Name	Description
Henry Ford Museum Greenville Village Dearborn, MI	Several presidential cars including the "Sunshine Special" and 1961/1964 Lincoln Parade Car
Imperial Palace Antique and Classic Auto Collection 3535 Las Vegas Blvd. Las Vegas, NV 89109	"Presidential Row Display" Cars used by Wilson, Roosevelt, Truman, Kennedy and Johnson
Little White House Historic Site Route 1; Box 10 Warm Springs, GA 31830	FDR's 1938 Ford and 1940 Willys with special controls
Museum of Automobiles Route 3, Box 306 Petit Jean Mountain Morrilton, AR	Clinton's Mustang
Pate Museum of Transportation Highway 377 between Forth Worth and Cresson PO Box 711 Fort Worth, TX 76101	Checker taxi used by Lee Harvey Oswald
Studebaker National Museum 525 South Main Street South Bend, IN 46601	Carriages used by Lincoln, Grant, Harrison and McKinley
Harry Truman Library U.S. Highway 24 and Delaware St. Independence, MO	Several cars used and/or owned by Truman

APPENDIX C

PRESIDENTIAL LIBRARIES

Jimmy Carter Presidential Library
One Copenhill Avenue
Atlanta, GA 30307-1498

Calvin Coolidge Memorial Room
Forbes Library
Northampton, MA 01060

Dwight D. Eisenhower Presidential Library
Abilene, KS 67410

Gerald R. Ford Presidential Library
1000 Beal Avenue
Ann Arbor, MI 48109-2114

The Hermitage: The Home of
  Andrew Jackson
4580 Rachel's Lane
Hermitage, TN 37076-1331

Herbert Hoover Presidential Library
Parkside Drive
West Branch, IA 52358

Lyndon Baines Johnson Presidential Library
2313 Red River Street
Austin, TX 78705

John F. Kennedy Presidential Library
Morrissey Blvd., Columbia Point
Boston, MA 02125

Lincoln Library
Springfield's Public Library
326 S. Seventh Street
Springfield, IL 62701

Richard M. Nixon Library & Birthplace
18001 Yorba Linda Blvd.
Yorba Linda, CA 92686

Ronald Reagan Presidential Library
40 President Drive
Simi Valley, CA 93065

Franklin D. Roosevelt Presidential Library
259 Albany Post Road
Hyde Park, NY 12538

Harry S. Truman Presidential Library
U.S. Highway 24 and Delaware Street
Independence, MO 64050

Research Library & Archives
Woodrow Wilson Birthplace Foundation
20 N. Coalter Street, Box 24
Staunton, VA 24401

INDEX